SHADES OF BLACK

The Origins

of Colour Consciousness

in the Caribbean

Clifford Hill
Alton Bell
Nigel Pocock

British Library Cataloguing in Publication Data:
a catalogue record for this publication
is available from the British Library

ISBN   978-1-912052-70-7

© Handsel Press 2022

The rights of Clifford Hill, Alton Bell and Nigel Pocock to be
identified as the authors of this work have been asserted
by them in accordance with the Copyright, Designs and
Patents Act 1988

Typeset in 11pt Calibri
at Haddington, Scotland

Printed by Bell and Bain, Glasgow
Cover design by WestPort Print and Design, St Andrews

Publisher's Note

It may seem strange for a Scottish Publishing House to bring out a book which is very largely concerned with London and parts of England which have a high proportion of residents whose parents or grandparents have come from Africa or the Caribbean. And although the book is very relevant to the present day, much of the content is about the 1960s and 1970s, when 'Britain' was often used loosely in contexts where 'England' might have been more accurate.

The book crosses two main genres – sociological analysis and memoir, and is also a tract for the times. This suits one of the aims of Handsel Press, which is to bridge the silos of modern life, and give popular books proper academic support.

One major reason for Handsel Press to be glad to own this book has come to light only in recent decades. Scots in the 20th century prided themselves on freedom from racist and anti-semitic attitudes which were thought to be only present down south. It is of course still true that Kenneth Kaunda made a pilgrimage to the headquarters of the Church of Scotland to give thanks for what Scottish Christians contributed towards Zambian independence. It is still true that a President of Israel once told an Assembly Moderator that Scotland was the one European country which lacked anti-semitism. And it is true that immigration to Scotland took place more slowly, and in cities like Dundee was more likely to include people from further east, because of the jute trade.

However, more recent research and writing has made it clear that many Scots shared the same racist and anti-semitic attitudes as many English, and that the Scots were as deeply involved in the slave trade and its profits as those in England. 'Jamaica' features in several Glasgow and Edinburgh street names, and it's said that there are more 'Camerons' in Jamaica than in Scotland! Iain Whyte's 2006 book may be entitled *Scotland and the Abolition of Black Slavery*, but it shares with other recent writing the recognition that Scotland was no less guilty than other parts of Britain.

An unusual feature of this book is the detailed reference to research away back in the 1960s. The author of, say, the Booker prizewinning novel of 2019, herself a person of colour, has written another book called *Blonde Roots* which imagines the slave trade reversed. She was born thirty years after the main author of *Shades of Black*, and explores quite different aspects of the African diaspora: but the colonial legacy is still with us, and Dr Hill's research, which is not easily accessed today, makes this a valuable documentary, combining academic analysis with 'stories from the times', even if a few of the 19th century books referred to are not fully referenced.

A less obvious virtue of an 'old' study like this is to remind us of how social attitudes really were back in the 1960s, as we now live in an age which unconsciously reads back modern assumptions into the past. The fact that one of the authors is himself an immigrant from Jamaica lends authenticity to the account. It is still true that most of the book is written by Clifford Hill, a white minister and sociologist, but Alton Bell, the black contributor, discussing the question of 'balance', had this to say:

> The issue of talking about slavery and its legacy or even tackling it among the black community is itself a challenge. Whilst growing up, we just accepted things the way they were and it was only when I left school and joined the workforce that I really encountered and became aware of overt racism. There are allies who really get it and understand the impact of racism on people of colour. Clifford Hill is one of those. Having worked, lived and associated with Caribbean people over many decades, he understands the unconscious trauma that we have inherited from our forebears, and has committed his life to help us change it. One could argue that he understands it better than some of our black folks.

Immigration is currently a matter reserved to the Westminster Government, and the same policy applies all over the UK. The detailed knowledge that Dr Hill and others share in this book, his sociological analysis of a key period of immigration to Britain, and his sharp illustrations of how this has played out in subsequent decades, makes this a book that will enlighten and challenge people in every part of the British Isles.

Black and White etc. are capitalised as nouns, and put in lower case as adjectives (but left as was in quotations).

CONTENTS

FOREWORD

The Black Lives Matter movement has stirred up all sorts of defensive anxieties; and recent developments around the fate of a memorial in a Cambridge college chapel to a benefactor involved in the Atlantic slave trade have produced a crop of interesting reactions of a defensive nature. The point is made that slavery was not a European invention and that there would not have been any victims of the Atlantic trade if it had not been for the existence of a slave trade within Africa, conducted by both Africans and Arab traders.

One thing that makes this response a morally and spiritually dubious one is that the first task of any serious individual or society – we might think – is surely to examine before God their own complicity or guilt, rather than to shift blame elsewhere. But there is a larger problem, one which this excellent book brings into very clear focus. Slavery is, alas, a worldwide phenomenon (and exists in all sorts of forms today); slavery, we are told, was practised by all kinds of societies and by people professing all kinds of religious faith. True; but there is something distinctive about the Atlantic slave trade.

Near the heart of its wickedness lay a set of beliefs about the intrinsic superiority of persons not only of a certain race but of a certain skin pigmentation. The slave trade succeeded in unleashing this corrupt and heretical view on the whole world and in 'canonising' that superiority in a way which continues to affect both global politics and domestic cultures. And because the institution of plantation slavery in the American colonies took for granted a monstrous level of predatory and exploitative sexual abuse towards enslaved persons, the issue of skin pigmentation became the subject of obsessive attention and categorisation within societies that had lived with the effects of slavery in the form of enforced 'mixed race' unions and their children. White prejudice managed to distort the power structures and status markers of non-white society by the bare fact of establishing white supremacy as an unquestionable norm, in ways that continued to organise the social pyramid around gradations of skin colour.

This is not the only long-term legacy of the Atlantic slave trade. This book charts in detail not only the complex story of the internal colour prejudice generated by slavery, but also the legacy of family disruption that narrowed the possibilities of so many Caribbean migrants to the UK from the 1950's onwards, and has increasingly damaged the lives and chances of so many younger people from these communities.

The point is that the Atlantic slave trade is not just one kind of slavery among others; its scale and its ongoing heritage make it a particularly corrosive and stubborn evil. The long-term effects of the trade in the Americas, in the Caribbean and in the UK are certainly diverse (and this book is clear about the different sorts of effects that need to be acknowledged and thought through), but what they have in common is the lasting capacity to ruin lives and destroy generations. It is appropriate that we recognise just why the Atlantic trade is so distinctive an evil – just as our forebears who fought the trade in the eighteenth century did (I am proud that one of my predecessors as Master of Magdalene College in Cambridge, Dr Peter Peckard, described the trade as a national sin inviting divine punishment, and used his influence in the university to encourage abolitionist arguments in its classrooms and pulpits).

There is so much to learn from the chapters in this book. They are well-researched, honest and deeply challenging. But perhaps where they speak most deeply is in addressing the defensiveness that I noted at the beginning of this introduction. We sometimes seem to behave and speak as though the admission of historical sin were a matter of humiliating weakness. But the Christian is bound to say that the truth sets us free, the truth that in Christ we are able to confront our own failure and transgression, with fear and trembling but not with despair or evasion. Admitting where we as societies and individuals have been wrong is a sign of strength and hope when it arises from a confidence that we have been shown the possibility of repentance and transformation. We should read this book with that kind of confidence – ready to accept how God calls us to new levels of struggle for his justice as he leads us to see how deeply we are entangled in injustice. That is the Good News that our authors seek to share as they tell the sad and shameful stories of our past inhumanities.

Rowan Williams

INTRODUCTION

The Movement for Justice and Reconciliation (MJR) that is linked with this book grew out of consultations held after the multi-ethnic riots in Tottenham and other areas of Britain in 2011. It was launched as a charity in September 2015 in St Mark's Kennington, followed by a presentation in the House of Lords. Its aim is to raise awareness of the legacies of colonial slavery and industrial exploitation by gathering existing, and commissioning new, research; making the findings known through educational projects and seeking to resolve injustice, promote wellbeing, and encourage community reconciliation in new and innovative ways.

MJR is a Christian organisation whose members believe it is God's unconditional, loving intention that all people, regardless of background, beliefs, ethnicity, gender, or sexuality, should have the right to justice, dignity, skills, equality, and an opportunity to work and hope for the future. The aim is to offer fresh life chances to those who have for too long been marginalised in society. See page 188 for contact details.

This book is an attempt to bring to public awareness the origins of colour consciousness rooted in colonial slavery, in the hope that this will provide a building block upon which greater understanding of relationships with black and other people of colour in a white dominated world can undergo fundamental changes of transformation that will relieve distress, bringing understanding and harmony in community relationships.

The writing of this book has been a unique experience that spans over half a century. It was back in the early 1960s that I carried out a small-scale study of colonial slavery in the Caribbean. This was prior to a visit to the West Indies sponsored by the British Council of Churches in 1962 and was linked with a study I did with the Institute of Race Relations in London entitled, 'West Indian Migrants and the London churches' published by Oxford University Press in 1963.

The objective of my initial study was more practical than academic. I had been working in London since 1952 with the first groups of worker-migrants from the Caribbean who are now known as the Windrush Generation. I was the minister of a busy inner-city church in a part of west London where many of the first-generation migrants were settling and were experiencing a range of social problems, particularly in the realm of housing accommodation and employment. In these two essential areas of life they were given no official assistance and I found myself actively helping them on an increasing, although unplanned, scale. I have given a brief description of some of my personal experience of working with the migrant communities in London in Chapters 2 and 4 of this book which gives some insight into the difficulties faced by the first settlers from the Caribbean.

The research on colonial slavery was simply intended to give me some background information before my visit to the West Indies, but it led to a desire to explore the origins of colour consciousness that I was meeting every day in London in both the black and white sectors of society. I wrote a lengthy paper on my research that was never published. I lost sight of it and forgot its existence until the first lockdown period of the coronavirus pandemic in 2020. I was searching for some old records of my work among people from the Caribbean in the Windrush Generation of the 1950s and 60s when I found the paper among a lot of other documents stored in a box in my loft. It was at the time when the 'Black Lives Matter' campaign became world news, following the untimely death of George Floyd at the hands of a white policeman in Minneapolis USA.

I sent copies of this research paper to some of my colleagues in MJR to see if they felt it was worth publishing. They encouraged me to re-work the paper into a broader setting of life among the migrant settlements in Britain where the legacy of slavery can be demonstrated against the background of community development of the overall migrant community that is now very much part of the British population.

The result of our discussions has been to produce this book together with the Revd Alton Bell who is now chairman of MJR and Nigel Pocock who was responsible for MJR's research programme at its inception. Alton has provided personal insights into life in Britain in contrast to his childhood in Jamaica. He describes his own transition from rural village life to that of a schoolboy in an inner-city part of London. Nigel's contribution is that of an academic researcher specialising in psychosomatic analysis and he provides some insightful observations that many readers will find illuminating.

My own work has been that of making my original research readable while putting it into the context of my personal experience of more than 60 years of living and working alongside people from the Caribbean islands and territories who have made their home in Britain. I have also carried overall editorial responsibility to ensure a continuity of investigating the origins of colour consciousness, particularly in Caribbean communities, both in the West Indies and among migrants in Britain. The first two chapters are from my pen, and then in Chapter 3, Alton Bell describes his experience of boyhood in Jamaica and Britain.

The facts derived from my original research paper with many quotations are used in the middle chapters of this book, particularly Chapters 6 to 10. It will, of course, be noted that many of the quotations in that section are derived from publications that were in print at that time and may no longer be available. Far from being a detraction, I believe it adds to the value of this book for research into the origins of colour consciousness and its roots in colonial slavery in the Caribbean. This is part of the legacy of slavery that is investigated in this book.

That legacy derives from the infamous Trade Triangle that lasted nearly 400 years, and was responsible for over 30 million men, women and children being violently removed from the African continent to provide the human capital to finance the Industrial Revolution in Britain and other parts of Europe and America. The Atlantic Trade Triangle was probably the greatest act of human exploitation in the history of the world. This Trade Triangle:

- Carried the produce of plantation slavery across to Europe providing sugar, rum, molasses, cotton, coffee and other goods required to stimulate and maintain the Industrial Revolution.
- Manufactured goods produced by the working poor in Britain were taken from Liverpool, Bristol, and London to be sold or bartered in Africa.
- Enabled them to be exchanged for the human cargo held in the slave castles along the West Coast of Africa. The cruelty and

inhumanity of the Middle Passage from Africa to the Americas and the Caribbean islands was notorious for its almost indescribable violence.

We can be sure that the white planters who ruled the sugar estates of the Caribbean islands and territories had no idea of the vast social issues they were creating for centuries to come when they seized African girls and raped them in the brutal days of colonial slavery. This is the subject of this book which the three of us have authored. It is our hope that it will encourage a sympathetic consideration of the heritage of the colonial era in British history that we believe to have great relevance for society today, and for improving race relationships.

It is our sincere hope in presenting this book to the public that it will make a significant contribution to understanding the issues that lie behind the passionate and sometimes violent protests of the 'Black Lives Matter' movement and other public demonstrations. The issues behind these protests are not easily grasped by the white population in Britain and other Western nations. It is for this reason that the black-and-white authorship of this book should open a window of understanding to issues of prejudice that are beyond rational explanation.

It is difficult for white people to enter into the experience of black and brown people who live in a white dominated world which appears to be the same world on the surface, but is in fact, a very different world for people of colour. To look at one instance – In the early 1970s I was living and working in the East End of London at the time when there was an outcry of protest against the police use of the 'stop and search' procedures which led to many unjust arrests and caused deep resentment in the black population. I was called out many times to go to the local police station to offer help to people I knew who had been detained under a variety of circumstances from mistaken identity to simply having been in the wrong place at the time.

Some outstanding cases that went into my notebook at that time included the black pastor of a local church who was arrested for running to catch a bus. I spoke to the arresting Constable who told me that when he sees a black man running, he knows "they're up to some no good". Young black men were many times more likely to be stopped when driving a car than white people. It was a very distressing time for the black community.

In Britain, statistics show a higher rate of criminal offences among the black Caribbean migrant populations than any other sector of society. There are more young African Caribbean men in British prisons than there are young African Caribbean men in our universities. White people see the statistics, but they do not know the stories behind them. They are particularly baffled by black-on-black violence, but they can never enter the world of the black or brown man who is trying to make his way in a white man's world, or the socially generated sense of inferiority that is often a driving force behind their behaviour.

This book is an attempt to put some of these things into perspective and to show the historical roots of some of the intractable social problems and irrational prejudices that have arisen in modern society that stemmed from 300 years of colonial slavery. This book is not part of an anticolonial campaign. It is simply an attempt, using the tools of social science and first-hand observation, to offer an historical and sociological perspective that may give greater understanding of current socially divisive issues.

Clifford Hill
April 2022

Chapter 1
EMPIRE AND COMMONWEALTH

This chapter is intended to provide a short introduction to the subject of the links between the British Empire and the British Commonwealth of Nations, with a short reference to the development of colonial slavery, its abolition and legacy. It puts this in the setting of current events in the development of the Commonwealth and the involvement of the Royal Family.

Harry and Meghan

The repercussions from the Oprah Winfrey interview with Harry and Meghan, the Duke and Duchess of Sussex, are likely to continue for many years. In the interview, broadcast to the world in March 2021, both Harry and Meghan referred to issues in their relationships within the Royal Family that involved racism. In the context of current culture debates, this is possibly the most explosive issue that could be raised. But the remark that referred to the issue was in itself quite innocuous. They both said that some unnamed person in the Royal Household had spoken about the colour of their first child when Meghan was expecting her first baby.

The question about the appearance of the baby would normally be heard in most families where there is speculation about whether the child will be more like his father or his mother, whether he or she will have blue or brown eyes, fair or dark hair. Of course, if there is a mixed-race element in the heritage of the parents, speculation will include skin colour. Such speculation need have no connection with racism at all. But both Harry and Meghan appeared to imply otherwise which increased tension with his family. It is, of course, a personal issue, and the Queen was perfectly right in responding that the family would deal with it as a private matter away from the public eye.

It should, however, be a matter of great public concern that the issue of racism in the history of Britain should be openly and honestly faced. Whether or not there are elements of prejudiced attitudes within the Royal Family is only of marginal importance, because they are human beings like the rest of the nation where there is plenty of evidence that such attitudes exist in the population. It would, therefore, be surprising if all members of the Royal Household were completely free of any form of racial prejudice.

It would appear that the initial joy of being accepted into the Royal family with its multitude of advantages and opportunities for public service began to evaporate for Meghan. From all the information available in the public arena it is impossible to know at what stage she began to feel stress, or what were the circumstances that led her to the point where she appeared unhappy with the British monarchy, as Giles Coran in *The Times* (13.03.21) suggested by playing both the mental health card and the race card. But Coran's suggestion is a good example of the despicable way some of the British press have treated Meghan which undoubtedly had its effect upon her mental health during difficult times in her first pregnancy.

Empire Legacy

There was, nevertheless, a point at which both Harry and Meghan may have initiated stress by poking the sleeping elephant in the room – colonial slavery! It was at a meeting with leaders of the Queen's Commonwealth Trust before they made public their desire to stand down from Royal duties. They each quite gently but firmly spoke about the past, saying that there were issues that really needed to be faced. They repeated this in their interview with Oprah Winfrey saying that there was a need to acknowledge the past and that everyone would benefit from such a review.

The problem here is that this statement raised confusion between things pertaining to the old British Empire and the Commonwealth. The Commonwealth does not have a history stretching back before 1949. The Commonwealth does not have an imperial past. But speaking at an online forum of the QCT in 2020 Harry spoke of the need for doing some soul-searching regarding the Commonwealth's imperial past and Meghan added that it would be uncomfortable. Harry actually said, "When you look across the Commonwealth, there is no way that we can move forward unless we acknowledge the past . . . and guess what, everybody benefits." Meghan added, "We are going to have to be a little uncomfortable right now, because it's only in pushing through that discomfort that we can get to the other side of this and find the place where the high tide raises all ships."

It is these innocent sounding remarks that would have frightened the British political establishment. The last thing they want is to make any links between the British Commonwealth and the imperial past of the old Empire. It is a reasonable assumption that this issue rather than any internal problems within the Royal Family is the most likely reason why the Queen found herself under pressure to remove the royal patronage of her Commonwealth Trust from Harry and Meghan when the end of their year of standing back from Royal duties was completed and they decided not to come back into the full role of family duties. It was certainly not something that the Queen would have wished to do, because she really wanted to see the injection of additional energy and a youthful understanding of contemporary issues that could be contributed by the Sussexes. It would appear that both Harry and Meghan went a little too quickly in raising issues from past history that would have to be faced at some stage, but there was preliminary work that needed to be done.

Black Lives Matter

The Queen herself has no political power and it is a golden rule in the House of Windsor that no one says anything to interfere with the political affairs of the nation. There is certainly no bigger political issue in Britain today than the legacy of slavery left over from the old British Empire. A supercharged racial atmosphere was generated by the 'Black Lives Matter' campaign following the murder of George Floyd in May 2020. In Britain this triggered the toppling of the statue of Edward Colston in Bristol, taking of the knee at football matches, and the impassioned protest marches in towns and cities, all of which exacerbated the situation.

Any discussion of the issue of slavery and the legacy it has left in parts of the Commonwealth, such as the Caribbean, became emotional rather than rational at this stage. For Harry and Meghan to sponsor such a discussion among Commonwealth leaders at this particular time when the economy had taken disastrous blows due to the Covid pandemic and the national lockdown restrictions would be found extremely difficult by the UK Government. It could, moreover, be seen as an unconstitutional interference by the monarchy into delicate political issues that would raise highly unwelcome legal problems.

Reparations

The last thing the UK Governments of any political party have wanted to face since the end of World War II is the issue of reparations for former colonial states who are now independent members of the British Commonwealth. It would undoubtedly bankrupt Britain if large financial sums were demanded in compensation for outstanding issues that were never faced at the time each of these Commonwealth nations achieved their independence. The rising public awareness of racial issues is slowly forcing onto the public agenda the issues of inequality that have characterised migrant populations in Britain since the 1950s and the advent of the Windrush Generation followed by the Indians and Pakistanis and others in the 1960s. These issues are slowly unravelling the web of restraint enforced by the political establishment in the UK against facing the existence of a legacy of slavery among Caribbean communities in Britain.

I have been involved in race relations since 1952 and I have been active in parliamentary circles since the 1960s; since the 1980s serving 25 years as the Convener of the Lords and Commons Family and Child Protection Group. This has given me considerable contact in both Houses of Parliament and many times I have raised issues of race relationships with MPs and peers. Always, the blockages appear immediately there is any mention of 'reparations' or even the recognition of the existence of a 'legacy of slavery'.

Research projects that I have been involved with have produced overwhelming evidence linking social problems found among Caribbean migrant communities in Britain to colonial slavery. But politicians of all parties simply do not want to know; or are totally unwilling to face these issues. If I have rightly understood Harry and Meghan, they are perfectly right in saying that unless these issues are faced, we will never be able to solve the intractable problems of social deprivation and inequality in migrant communities in Britain. But maybe in these days of Covid crisis they cannot be faced without endangering the economic stability of much of the world.

Race and Ethnic Disparities Report

A Government sponsored report on 'Race and Ethnic Disparities' published on 31 March 2021, contained a section on 'cultural traditions, family, and integration'.[1] The report quoted ONS figures for family and marriage which showed that a total of 14% of families in the UK were led by a single-parent (2.9 million). But 63% of black Caribbean children in Britain are said to be growing up in single-parent families. The fact that is of even greater significance than the fatherlessness of these children is that 43% of African children are in single-parent families. The report gives a number of possible reasons for the high level of family breakdown in these African and Caribbean groups such as poverty, living conditions, and socio-economic factors. But no one appears to have noted that although the African figures for one parent families are three times as high as the national average, the Caribbean figures are almost five times as high as the national average.

It is the difference between the African and Caribbean figures that is of the greatest sociological significance, where the one major variable between the two is the factor of colonial slavery. This was never experienced by the Africans but is of major sociological significance in the history of the Caribbean migrants in Britain. It will surely have to be faced one day and it is a reasonable deduction to conclude that this was the issue that Harry and Meghan were trying to raise in their conversations with Commonwealth leaders.

The Commonwealth

The Queen herself has taken a great interest in the Commonwealth, right from the beginning of her long reign and she has shown enormous sympathy and sensitivity for diversity issues and the encouragement of greater understanding between different nations and communities.

His Royal Highness the late Duke of Edinburgh fully shared the Queen's concern for racial equality in the British Commonwealth. This was demonstrated in the vast number of young people who have benefited from the Duke of Edinburgh Awards that has

---

1   Report of the Government Commission on Race and Ethnic Disparities published 31st March 2021.

opened up new life changing opportunities for people of all racial backgrounds in more than 140 nations. My wife and I were among the first guests to be invited to St George's House in Windsor Castle to explore issues of race relations in 1966. We were greatly impressed by Prince Philip's commitment to seeking ways of applying his Christian faith to the issues of combating racial prejudice.

Diversity and Equality

The formation of the British Commonwealth of Nations in 1949 marked a huge step away from the old days of Empire and white domination. The Queen herself has taken a great interest in fostering relationships between the different parts of the Commonwealth and the formation of a family of nations with a common purpose, not merely of encouraging trade, but in building relationships of support for mutual benefit. Diversity and equality have been central to the development of the Commonwealth and there can be no doubt that the Queen was genuinely delighted to welcome Meghan into the Royal Family as Harry's wife. She clearly saw the great advantage of having in the Royal Family someone of mixed heritage and Meghan's mother was given a special welcome at the wedding celebrations in May 2018. It was an opportunity to move away from the repressive days of Empire into a new era of equality and mutual respect in a Commonwealth of Nations.

Queen's Commonwealth Trust

A month before Harry and Meghan's wedding there was a meeting of Commonwealth Heads of Government in London. The Queen had already decided to bestow the honour on the young couple of being the President and Vice President of the Queen's Commonwealth Trust (QCT). They were officially introduced to Commonwealth leaders at a meeting in the Queen Elizabeth II Conference Centre, Westminster, on 18 April 2018. No doubt the Queen saw this as a huge opportunity for younger members of her family to play a key role in the development of the Commonwealth that had been dear to her heart even before her own marriage and becoming Queen.

Relationships between the Queen and Meghan were extremely warm at this stage and Meghan describes travelling in the car between meetings when the Queen shared the rug over her knees with Meghan, drawing her closer beside her. They appeared together at these meetings, sharing warmly in the events with both of them completely at ease with each other. There can be no doubt that Meghan, despite being an American divorcee of mixed racial heritage, was fully accepted into the Royal family at that stage.

It is quite impossible, from what has been put into the public arena, to know at which point things began to go wrong in the relationship between Meghan and the Royal family. In her interview with Oprah Winfrey, Meghan referred to her mental health problems, to feeling lonely and unsupported, and that she had asked for help, but it was not received. No information was given as to the circumstances that gave rise to these feelings although, of course, it gave plenty of room for tabloid speculation which has been unhelpful and must have considerably increased the level of stress for both Harry and Meghan.

Legal Issues

Commonwealth leaders have a strong track record of promoting equality in diversity. The pressures put upon South Africa in the fight against apartheid displayed to the world the commitment of the British Commonwealth to the acceptance of racial equality. This was matched by the swiftness in Britain of enacting laws against discrimination in public places and in employment in the early days of Commonwealth migration in the 1960s. This was a public declaration of the values of equality that are enshrined in British law. But these values have not always been there, as any honest evaluation of the history of the British Empire soon reveals.

The foundations of the Race Relations Acts of the 1960s actually go back to the 18th century and the 'Mansfield Declaration' of 1772, which prevented a runaway slave, James Somerset, from being returned from Britain to Virginia. Many people took this as a licence for freedom – and in Scotland it led to the freeing of one Joseph Knight in 1788 (from 'perpetual servitude' rather than 'slavery' – a technicality which allowed the Lord Advocate, Henry Dundas, to say in 1776 that there were 'no slaves in Britain') – but the canny Lord Mansfield said that by his judgment he wished 'all the masters in England to think their slaves were free and all the slaves to think they were not'![2] However, the declaration was a milestone on the route to the abolition of the slave trade in 1807 and the final emancipation of all enslaved persons throughout the British Empire that was enacted in 1833.

The abolition of slavery was probably the longest and most bitterly fought Parliamentary battle of all time, beginning with a small group of campaigners in the late 18th century such as Thomas Clarkson and Granville Sharp. They were joined by William Wilberforce whose life's ambition was to change the values of the nation. He wrote in his diary on Sunday, 28 October 1787:

> God Almighty has set before me two great objects, the suppression of the slave trade and the reformation of manners (moral values).[3]

Wilberforce knew the extent of the battle to change moral and spiritual values, because throughout Britain in the 18th century it had become increasingly fashionable for 'families of quality' to have black African coachmen, footmen, and other servants.

The difficulties of employing Africans who had been slaves in the colonies even before their legal emancipation in Britain in 1771, was clearly expressed by a writer in the *Gentleman's Magazine* in the year 1764:

> The practice of importing negro servants into these kingdoms is said to be alreadie a grievance that requires a remedy, and yet it is every day encouraged, insomuch that the number in this metropolis only, is supposed to be near 20,000:[4] the main objection to their importation is that they cease to consider themselves as slaves in this free country, nor will they put up with an inequality of treatment, nor more willingly perform the laborious duties of servitude than our own people, and if put to it, are generally sullen, spiteful,

---

2 See Iain Whyte, *Scotland and the Abolition of Black Slavery, 1756-1838*, Edinburgh University Press, Edinburgh 2007, 16-24.

3 Quoted in Clifford Hill, *The Wilberforce Connection,* Monarch Books, Oxford 2004, 49.

4 This is almost certainly an inflated figure. Olaudah Equiano estimated that there were about 14,000 men and women of African descent scattered around England in 1777. This is stated in Angelina Osborne: *Equiano's Daughter,* Momentum Arts, Cambridge, 2007, 2.

treacherous and revengeful. It is therefore highly impolitic to introduce them as servants here where that rigour and severity is impracticable which is absolutely necessary to make them useful.[5]

It is clear that prejudiced attitudes towards people of African descent were already deeply entrenched in Britain by this time. In fact, those attitudes go even farther back in history as the first Race Relations Act controlling immigration was not passed in the reign of Queen Elizabeth II in 1962, but during the reign of Queen Elizabeth I in 1596. It was worded thus:

Her Majestie, understanding that there are of late divers blackmoores brought into this realme, of which kinde of people there are alreadie too manie, consideringe how God hath blessed this lande with great increase of people of our owne nation . . . Those kinde of people should be sent forth from the lande.[6]

Institutional Prejudice

John Wesley recognised the extent to which prejudiced attitudes had become embedded in British culture when he wrote to Wilberforce what is believed to be the last letter before his death, encouraging Wilberforce to go on with the campaign for the abolition of slavery. He wrote:[7]

Unless the divine power has raised you up to be an *Athanasius contra mundum* I cannot see how you can go through with your glorious enterprise in opposing that execrable villainy which is the scandal of religion, of England and of human nature. Unless God has raised you up for this very thing, you will be worn out by the opposition of men and devils; but if God is with you, who can be against you? Are all of them stronger than God? Oh, do not be weary in well doing. Go on, in the name of God

---

5 *The Gentleman's Magazine*, Volume XXXIV, 1764, 492; quoted in Clifford Hill, *Immigration and Integration: a study of the settlement of coloured minorities in Britain*, Pergamon Press, Oxford 1970,

6 Acts of The Privy Council, 11 August 1596, quoted in Clifford Hill, *How Colour Prejudiced is Britain?* Victor Gollancz Ltd, London 1965, 22.

7 Hill, *The Wilberforce Connection,* 53.

and in the power of his might, till even American slavery, the vilest that ever saw the sun, shall vanish away before it. That he who has guided you from your youth up, may continue to strengthen you in this and in all things, is the prayer of dear Sir, your affectionate servant

John Wesley (24 February 1791)

It is, of course, far easier to pass a law making it illegal to exercise discrimination in the public arena than to change the attitudes of prejudice that lead to discrimination. On the positive side, the laws of a nation represent a public declaration of national values and the personal and corporate values that underlie racial awareness and attitudes between diverse communities. Changing attitudes is a matter of huge complexity, but legal requirements that establish standards of behaviour in public undoubtedly have an effect upon personal values, even if those changes only take place slowly over a long period of time.

Changing Attitudes

The first step on the road to making fundamental changes in the attitudes of a population has to be the recognition of the need for a change. If there is no awareness of the problem, there will be no challenge to the *status quo* and life will go on from generation to generation with unjust practices becoming systemically institutionalised. That was the situation in the British Empire in the late 18th century after 300 years of slavery. The practice of transporting captured Africans from the West Coast of Africa to the Americas and the Caribbean islands and territories became firmly institutionalised by the late 15th and early 16th century.

In 1455 Pope Nicholas V had given Portugal the right to take African captives in territories south of the Sahara and reduce them to perpetual slavery. British involvement began in 1662 when John Hawkins sailed to West Africa and took a cargo of Africans to St Domingo. The infamous Trade Triangle developed soon after this with Britain gradually becoming dominant in the West Indies, taking Barbados from the Dutch and Trinidad and Jamaica from the Spanish. The British developed sugar plantations employing large numbers of Africans until the abolition of the slave trade in 1807, but during those years more than 3 million Africans are estimated to have been transported across the Atlantic.

Abolitionist Movements

Strong abolitionist movements did not make much headway in Britain until the second half of the 18th century by which time slavery had become an important part of the British economy fuelling the Industrial Revolution. If lone voices were raised against the trade, intellectual arguments were offered in justification, even to the extent that Africans were said to be of a different species of humanity from Europeans.

If consciences were stirred against the slave trade and the practices of slavery on the plantations, they were overruled by economic considerations. Slavery had become so endemic in the British economy that by the end of the 18th century some two thirds of the national GDP was said to be linked in some way with slavery. This, of course, did not justify the vile practices of the Trade Triangle and the actions of the plantocracy, but it was sufficient to influence the debates in Parliament and to frustrate the work of the abolitionists for several decades. In fact, Wilberforce was on his deathbed when he heard that Parliament had finally agreed to the abolition of slavery throughout the British Empire in 1833 – some 50 years since he had made the abolition of slavery the dominant objective of his life.

African Involvement

William Wilberforce and his friends in the Clapham Group were not the only ones responsible for achieving the abolition of slavery: all too often the efforts of the Africans themselves are overlooked. Not only were there well-known black activists such as Olaudah Equiano and Ottobah Cugoano in Britain who were tireless in campaigning for The Society for Effecting the Abolition of the Slave Trade (SEAST), but in the West Indies there were numerous slave uprisings and increasing unrest that created problems for the authorities. These were often brutally suppressed which increased the spirit of resentment and the longing for freedom among the enslaved Africans. Many of the Africans on the plantations lost their lives or were cruelly beaten for taking part in demonstrations in the period between the abolition of the slave trade in 1907 and the final setting free of all slaves that was not concluded until 1838.

It is this lack of recognition of the important part played by the Africans themselves in the struggle for the abolition of slavery that is a matter of deep resentment today. The film 'Amazing Grace', released at the time of the 200th anniversary of the abolition of the slave trade in 2007, showed the insensitivity to white superiority that is institutionalised in both American and British culture. The film featured the work of William Wilberforce as the great hero of abolition together with his white companions, and with only a brief mention of Olaudah Equiano as the only black man in the film, which ended with the triumphant playing of the Scots Guards giving the impression that a great victory had been won and there were no more problems of race relationships.

Emancipation Act 1833

However, what the film 'Amazing Grace' did not mention was the incredible injustice of the 1833 abolition that granted a payment of £20 million of British taxpayers' money to be given to the owners of slaves in compensation for the loss of their property and the income from their slave labour. But at the same time no provision was made for the Africans in the Caribbean islands and territories who were set free. They were simply given their freedom to look after themselves and provide for themselves and their children in whatever way they could find, which meant for most of them a life of grinding poverty.

In the eyes of the people in the West Indies the 1833 Emancipation Act was a monumental injustice which rewarded British citizens who owned African slaves, but not a single penny was paid to the Africans themselves who were set free but given no help in providing their own livelihoods.

For nearly 200 years this scandalous injustice has not been publicly discussed. Not only has this issue been kept away from public debate, but the history of colonial slavery itself has not been taught in many British state schools. In my own experience, if history lessons contained any reference to slavery, it would usually be taught in terms of the cotton fields of America, with no mention of the sugar plantations of the British Caribbean.

The Zong Exhibition

More than half the white British people visiting the Zong slave ship exhibition in 2007 had little or no knowledge of colonial slavery. The 200th anniversary of the abolition of the slave trade was marked by bringing an 18th century replica sailing ship into London. It was moored alongside Tower Pier, adjacent to the Tower of London, with an exhibition of colonial slavery in All Hallows by the Tower. A questionnaire was given to visitors which was completed by more than 6000 respondents. The first question was designed to discover how much people already knew about slavery before coming to the exhibition. Less than half of all the visitors (41%) had been taught about slavery in school. This, of course, does not mean that 41% of those attending had a detailed knowledge of colonial slavery, it was simply an indication of visitors' awareness of Britain's involvement in slavery in the period leading up to the abolition of the slave trade. Moreover, all these respondents were people with sufficient interest in the subject to pay to attend the Zong project, so they were not necessarily a cross section of the public.

Just over half of those attending were white British (53%), 28% were from the Caribbean and 7% were Africans, 10% were other nationalities and 2% did not give their ethnic origins. In response to questions about the transatlantic slave trade only 37% of white British people showed any knowledge. This was in contrast to 62% of people from the Caribbean and 46% of Africans.

80% of Africans and Caribbeans said that they had learned a lot by attending the Zong exhibition and 91% of white British also said they had learned a lot. In order not to rely upon the subjective evidence of personal self-assessment or the educational value of the project, the survey included an additional question. This was designed to provide empirical evidence of the knowledge gained by respondents through their visit to the Zong Project. The question, on a before and after basis, used the names of prominent abolitionists together with some bogus names such as Oliver Cromwell. This showed significant increase in knowledge in regard to all the abolitionists, with particular increase in the cases of Olaudah Equiano, Thomas Clarkson, and Hannah More.

Knowledge of Colonial Slavery

The issues surrounding the ending of the slave trade in 1807 and the banning of the practice of slavery throughout the British Empire in 1838 have never been a subject widely taught in British state schools or of parliamentary debate. The terms on which the African Caribbeans were released from slavery has never been a subject of public discussion. The results of the survey and numerous conversations with the public at the Zong Project showed almost no awareness of conditions in the Caribbean at the end of slavery.

For the African Caribbeans, the situation has never been faced that they were deprived, not only of their freedom, but of their identity, their language, their culture, and their heritage, and even their names. It should surely have been a matter of prudence as well as justice to have invested in some form of economic development and training programmes for the newly freed Africans. Of course, in 1833 schools had not been established in England for all children, it would be another 40 years before education was extended to all children, but the Industrial Revolution was in full swing in Britain and some of the manufacturing processes could have been established in the Caribbean together with some form of occupational training. Instead, people were left to scrape a living from a small parcel of land if they were fortunate enough to be able to obtain such ownership, or to hire themselves to those who did manage to obtain land.

This lack of any provision for the former slaves resulted in generations of grinding poverty for most of the population in the Caribbean islands and territories. It was this situation that was the drive behind the migration to Britain of large numbers in the 1950s and 60s more than a hundred years after the ending of slavery. But the political issues in regard to compensation have never been examined.

David Cameron's Visit

No one in government wants to start to unpack these highly charged issues involved in a review of colonial slavery, although there have been increasing calls for such a review for a number of years. There were high hopes that the issues were at last going to be faced when David Cameron was Prime Minister and he paid a visit to Jamaica in 2015, as the first British Prime Minister to do so.

14

He told the Jamaican people that Britain was prepared to set aside a large sum of money for a construction project. But the project was not to build schools, or a new university, or to invest in industrial development that would provide much-needed jobs.

The proposal David Cameron took to Jamaica was that the British Government would build a huge prison on the island. But even this would not be for the benefit of Jamaica, but to relieve the pressure on British prisons by sending to Jamaica those of Jamaican heritage convicted of felony in Britain so that they could serve their term of incarceration on Jamaican soil. There was not even the pretence of saying that this was going to be of great social benefit to Jamaica. It was purely a self-serving proposal to help the British penal service.

Colour Consciousness

There is, however, an even greater issue of injustice arising out of colonial slavery which is the unmentionable subject of colour differentiation. No one wants to discuss this. But it is at the heart of so many of the problems faced by people in the Caribbean and those of Caribbean descent in other parts of the world, and of black people in the southern states of the USA where slavery was practised.

The issue that has never been faced in Britain is the ***origins* of the colour code differentiation** which is the subject being examined in this book. It is a subject of the most subtle and yet most pernicious form of discrimination that does not just affect people on the island of Jamaica or the other Caribbean territories. It affects millions of black and brown people scattered across the globe, and this is the issue that we want to investigate in this book.

Chapter 2
THE WINDRUSH GENERATION

The purpose of this chapter is to set the scene of the settlement of the Windrush Generation of the 1950s and 1960s in Britain. It looks at the development of race and colour consciousness in Britain beginning at that time, and then Clifford Hill gives some first-hand accounts of the social issues confronting the first migrants as they developed communities in West London. Other issues faced by the migrants involved their faith and expectations before migration.

Black Lives Matter

The 'Black Lives Matter' movement that had its origins several years earlier burst onto the world scene in May 2020. It was not just an expression of outrage against the killing of a black man by a white policeman in Minneapolis USA, it was a revelation of the underlying frustration of people of African origin living in Western nations where the vast majority of them form an underclass with all the sociological characteristics of a caste in the lack of social mobility. In the USA, it is within the lifetime of most people still living that the civil rights movement achieved the abolition of segregation in the southern United States that had dominated most areas of public life, from travelling on a bus to primary school and college education. Segregation has been banned by law, but attitudes of white superiority are harder to banish.

The action of a white policeman kneeling on the neck of a black man suspected of some criminal action, even to the point of causing his death, would have gone unnoticed a generation ago before smart phones with their cameras were available. The video went viral and formed the centrepiece of evidence in the prosecution of Derek Chauvin who was found guilty of murder in an unprecedented verdict of a white policeman being convicted in Minneapolis USA. Whether or not this will prove to be the beginning of a major change in police relationships with black communities in the US is still very much in the balance, but the verdict undoubtedly saved many US cities being plunged into a period of racial turmoil and destruction. Police tactics in some parts of the USA have changed little since the days when they captured runaway slaves and returned them to their owners in the South or hung them on the street corners. But the new factor is the raising of public awareness and the widespread desire for fundamental changes to take place.

The situation in Britain has some basic differences from the USA. There has never been racial slavery on the soil of the United Kingdom, although its citizens practiced slavery in British Overseas Territories for 300 years. So why was there such a passionate outpouring of rage in Britain and other Western nations when the video film of the killing of George Floyd was widely distributed through social media and news media including mainstream television? It surely demonstrated the existence of something much more powerful than indignation about a single act of injustice. In fact, it exposed a mountain of unresolved social issues in race relationships between people of colour and the white majority in these nations. They were issues that were only barely below the surface.

Early Days

Our concern here is with the situation in Britain, and primarily England. Until halfway through the 20th century, race relationships was not an issue with the British public. For 300 years, until 1 August 1838, the British were actively involved in some form of slavery in British Overseas Territories. But the British public had no first-hand experience of slavery based on colour or internal racial issues. Awareness of the cruelty of slavery in the colonies did not become a major public issue until the later years of the 18th century and the abolition activities of people like Clarkson, Equiano, Hannah More and Wilberforce.

The Act of Emancipation passed by Parliament in London in 1833 was followed by five years of so-called 'apprenticeship' in the Caribbean islands until the African slaves were finally given their freedom; but with no compensation for all that they had lost – most of all for their lost identity as sons and daughters of Africa. The unspeakable cruelty that the African victims of slavery had endured was given no recognition in their emancipation. This monumental injustice, noted in Chapter One, was reinforced by the vast sum of money paid to their owners in Britain in compensation for losing the income from the forced labour of the slaves. This injustice was given no public recognition in Britain until it was brought to notice by a piece of research undertaken by the Legacies of British Slavery (LBS) based at University College London in 2013.

Until the outbreak of the Second World War 'British Empire Day' was a public holiday enthusiastically celebrated as a national bank holiday event. After the Second World War, which was immediately followed by a succession of colonies achieving their independence, there were valiant efforts to celebrate Commonwealth Day – a much more acceptable concept to the liberal minded – but it never quite caught the public imagination as the old Empire Day had done.

Race and Colour Consciousness

Pride of race and national self-consciousness such as we see expressed in many parts of the world today are by no means newly emergent concepts of society. Twentieth Century German ideas of a 'master race' were not unique in the history of humanity. Such concepts are familiar to the student of Greek or Roman history and are even implicit in the racial exclusiveness of the people of Israel from the time of Moses, more than a thousand years before Christ.

What *is* a new aspect of racial awareness, is the emergence during the early years of the 20th century, of the understanding of 'double consciousness' among black and brown peoples of the world. This is the experience among fair skinned people of identifying with the white people in society in terms of their values and aspirations, but being regarded as black, due to their mixed racial ancestry. About the same time 'Colour Consciousness' became a racial issue in the USA and soon after the middle of the century, in the post-World War II period, it also became an issue in Britain. In the USA distinctions between black and white people have been part of the structure of society since the early days of slavery with Africans being imported from Africa that began in AD 1619.

In Britain it was not until the arrival in June 1948 of about 500 immigrants[7] from the Caribbean, aboard the *'Empire Windrush'* that the presence of people of colour came to the notice of the British public. Most of these incomers were men, some of whom had served

---

7 The Windrush Foundation has now put this fugure at 1027, from landing cards.

in the British armed forces during the Second World War. They had fond memories of Britain and faced with widespread unemployment and poverty in the Caribbean, they took advantage of their British passports to make the journey from Kingston, Port of Spain, and other Caribbean capitals to Tilbury in the hope of finding a better life.

There were two push factors that encouraged the emigration from the West Indies in the earliest days of the post-World War II migration. They were the disastrous hurricane of 1951 that hit Jamaica very badly, and the second push factor was the passing of the McCarran Act 1952 in the USA that tightened restrictions on the entry of migrant labour from the Caribbean. Until that time it had been a regular practice for men from the West Indies to go to the USA for fruit picking and other harvesting on a short-term basis, but this was virtually stopped in 1952 so that the men began looking for other places for employment and for a better standard of life.

Problems for Newcomers

That hope was rudely shattered for most of the newcomers by the reality of life in Britain. I lived and worked among this first-generation of Caribbean migrants in West London in the early 1950s and I saw the hardships that they endured, especially in finding accommodation and work and being able to survive in the depths of an English winter. Like the rest of the white population, I knew nothing about the background of our new neighbours, or of their cultural mores.

Although I was a Londoner and I had spent the whole of my boyhood in London in the 1930s, I don't remember ever seeing a black person. During the war we saw some of them in the American armed forces posted to Britain, but I did not meet any of them face-to-face. After the war, in 1947 I was called up to do my National Service and then while still on demob leave, I went straight up to university to read theology and prepare for my life's work in ministry. I was ordained in 1952 and began work in my first pastorate in Harlesden, north-west London, where many of the first wave of what later became known as the 'Windrush Generation' were settling.

In the first week of my working life, a young man from Jamaica came to see me asking if I would conduct a wedding for him. I visited the address he gave me to find him already living with the young lady who was to be his bride. They occupied one room in a multi-occupied house filled with similar black immigrants, with several of whom I had conversations. This began what rapidly became a major part of my pastoral ministry in London. It was the beginning of my contact with non-white people.

I soon discovered that the major problems confronting this first-generation of Caribbean immigrants was the search for jobs and for accommodation. Both of these issues presented major hurdles for the newcomers for whom there were no official centres where they could go for help and advice – there was no immigration centre giving them helpful advice on steering their way through the maze of official regulations and social customs that most British people take for granted.

Of course, they visited the local employment exchange, but many of the newcomers found that their skills did not match the requirements of jobs in the local area. When they went searching for somewhere to rent a room, they found even greater difficulties with many of them being told quite openly by white landlords that they did not take black tenants. The corner shop windows with notices for rooms to let, invariably said 'No Coloured' on their adverts.

Church Attendance

In the West Indies I had seen churches of all the mainline denominations filled with enthusiastic worshippers and eager participation in church events. My enquiries showed that roughly 70% of the population in Jamaica attended church of one or another of the main denominations similar to those we have in Britain. Also, to my surprise, only about 5% of the churchgoing population attended Pentecostal churches.

In September 1965 I published an article in *The Congregational Monthly* entitled 'Colour in Britain' in which I said:

> One of the saddest features of the present period of immigration from the Commonwealth, is the very large fall-off in church attendance that has taken place amongst coloured Christians who have settled in Britain. In a survey of churches of all denominations carried out in London during 1963, it was revealed that only 4% of West Indians living in the London area, attend church on Sundays. This compares with 69% in the West Indies.

I added: 'It would be wrong to lay the whole blame for this widespread loss of faith upon the English churches. It is due rather to the **total** impact of the migration to Britain upon the lives of the immigrants.' In a further reference in the same article, I said:

> The migrants from the Caribbean find life in Britain extremely tiring and usually go to bed much earlier than most English people, at least during the weekdays. At the weekend they do their shopping and household chores. On Sundays they are often too tired to make the effort to go to church. Many of them have to work on Sundays – a thing unheard-of before coming to Britain.

This reminded me of a letter I had received from a Jamaican migrant in the early days of the Windrush group in 1953. It was from an address in London W.1 which I quoted in my first book on the subject. It read:

> Dear Minister,
>
> Please accept usual greetings in Jesus' sweet and holy name. So, I am indeed sorry to know that I never had the privilege yesterday evening to come to service, through having to go to work. Only the dear Lord knows my feelings towards that. Anyway, I truly know by the grace of God, He is going to open the way for me that I shall be able to go to church more often.
>
> I could remember Sundays back home, preaching to hundreds of people. I thank you very much, Sir, for that love and mercy you have for us, the coloured. God bless you, and I know that the dear Lord will reward you. I believe, by God's grace I will be there on Sunday evening at church, and I am trying to bring some friends along with me. Please remember me in your prayers.
>
> I am yours in the Master's service.[8]

There were many other reasons for this greatly reduced church attendance by the first generation of Caribbean migrants, the majority of whom were used to being in church regularly back in the West Indies. One of the strongest reasons was that they soon discovered that only a small minority of English people actually were going to

---

8 Quoted in: Clifford Hill, *Black and White in Harmony, The Drama of West Indians in the Big City from a London Minister's Notebook*, with a Foreword by Trevor Huddleston, Hodder and Stoughton, London 1958, 24.

church in the areas where they were living and working. In the inner-city areas where most of the migrants settled, church attendance was extremely low and there were many stories circulating amongst the migrants that when they did visit a particular church, they were not made welcome. This was a shock to the newcomers, not only to their faith, but to the high regard they held for Britain and the British people prior to immigration.

Certainly, some of the stories in circulation were true. A man in my congregation told me that he had been turned away when he visited a nearby Anglican church. I checked with the vicar of that church who remembered the incident; but said that he had simply advised the man that he would probably be more comfortable at my church where many West Indians were reported to attend, than in his church where there were no other black people. However kindly the vicar's advice may have been, it was certainly interpreted as meaning, 'Please don't come here again.'

In the early days I heard many stories from the West Indian members of my congregation of incidents at work where they had been scorned for singing a hymn or reading their Bibles during a tea break or speaking about God in the presence of their workmates. They soon discovered that any expression of their Christian faith or admitting that they go to church brought scorn and derision. They realised that by going to church they would be hindering their acceptance by English people and their integration into society. To let it be known that they were Christians worshipping God only served to increase their minority status.

Maintaining the Faith

Of course, those who had a strong faith were able to maintain their Christian commitment despite the scorn of workmates. Those who came to our church were from different denominational traditions. In the early days of the 1950s our objective was simply to respond to needs. Within a few weeks of my ordination in 1952 a young man who had been attending our church for a few weeks bought a young lady on Sunday morning introducing her to me and asking if I would marry them. I discovered that she had been an evangelist in Jamaica and that they both attended the Pentecostal 'Church of God in Christ'.

This was my first encounter with Pentecostals, and I was impressed by the strength of their faith. Our white congregation soon took this young couple to their hearts and decided, as a wedding present, to give them the reception, which was arranged in the church hall. This was a time of great rejoicing as white and coloured Christians joined in a party after the wedding reception which followed the service in the church. Their week's honeymoon was spent in our home in the church house, after which they returned to their one room dwelling on the third floor of a large house in Kilburn which they shared with a number of other migrant families. We were always grateful for that week in which we were privileged to enter closely into the lives of these two Christian young people. We learned much about their background and their life in Jamaica before coming to Britain which was of great use in the ministry we were to exercise.

Finding Employment

One of the major problems facing the first generation of migrants was in finding jobs that were appropriate to their skills. I became quite an expert in helping them to find employment. With each one I would go through a regular routine of questions and in time I became quite experienced at screening them and placing them in suitable jobs. I would scan the employment columns of the local newspaper and build up a list of employers who were willing to take coloured labour. A few employers would not engage them on principle, while others excused themselves on the ground that they feared trouble either from the Unions or from their English employees.

On the whole, the majority of employers received my enquiries kindly and proved willing to take on suitable men – if they had the vacancies. Several firms became my regular customers and their personnel managers used to telephone and describe the job they had vacant and ask for a suitable man. All these firms spoke of the dependability of the Jamaican worker who, although sometimes slower than their English counterpart, was nevertheless thorough in his work. One firm in Wembley would only take coloured workers if they came through me and I had the strange experience of having a number of Jamaicans call to say that they had applied for a job there but were told that they could only be considered if they had a letter from me. Among my congregation the church house was known as

'The Jamaican Labour Exchange'. The following letter is typical of many such notes received from the ever-increasing number of West Indians who came to the church:

Dear Mr Hill

Precious greetings to you in the name of Jesus. This is to say that I was unable to be in church on Sunday. I went to see a young man who is sick. My friend is living in Lewisham and he is desirous of living down here with his brother, so he has asked me to get a job at my works. I saw the foreman and he said, 'Yes, there is a job' but I am to send him to you.

With thanks I am

C . . . J . . .

All the migrants with whom I came into contact were keen and eager to work, but there were many problems, particularly for semi-skilled workers whose skills did not quite fit into the labour market in Britain. Quite a few of the first generation from the West Indian islands came from rural backgrounds for whom industrial jobs presented a whole new world, but there was generally an eagerness to learn new skills and a determination to make adjustments in their lifestyle. There were, inevitably, particular problems for those who lacked basic educational skills. A small number of men were illiterate and therefore faced particular difficulties in industry where they could not read notices about danger and the use of machinery.

In order to deal with the problems of these men, Monica, my wife, set up literacy classes on a very private and confidential basis in our church hall. The men were obviously sensitive to their situation and while they needed help, they did not want others to know. This was not publicly advertised and was only made known by word of mouth and was tailored to suit their needs of employment. We started with just one or two men who passed on the invitation to other men who were in a similar position.

Although Monica was an experienced teacher, her experience had been entirely with schoolchildren albeit teenagers, and she had to make radical changes to adapt to adult education, which she did with great sensitivity, and we made many long-term friends. It was not easy to find reading material that suited their particular needs, but this was done, and the men were greatly appreciative, and each made a lot of progress which was very gratifying.

A Polite Generation

The Windrush Generation were mainly men, whose intention was to come to Britain to find work for a limited number of years and then return home. This had been the custom with migrant labour from the Caribbean islands going to the USA with work permits up to three years, but this had recently been stopped which is one of the reasons why those who found it hard to make a living in the Caribbean turned to Britain.

We found the vast majority of this first-generation to be polite, hard-working, and trustworthy. They were incredibly patient in coping with the overt prejudice against their presence among local people. They endured the hardships of searching for accommodation and employment with great fortitude and good humour that certainly won our admiration. They coped amazingly with the hardships of the British winter and the flimsy clothing they had brought with them. Usually, the only heating in the rooms they were able to rent came from paraffin stoves with the inevitable smell permeating the house.

Social Problems

The only social problems they caused were the occasional house parties celebrating a family gathering, a wedding or a christening. Sometimes this would go on late into the night with windows open on warm summer days. Of course, the noise from the inevitable radiogram with Caribbean music could be heard by most of the street that prompted complaints to the police. The local police were always nervous of intervening and on a number of occasions they called me out in the early hours of the morning. I would go straight into the house and speak to whoever was organising the party asking for the volume to be turned right down and on every occasion, I was politely obeyed, and a potentially explosive social conflict was avoided.

My reputation began to spread rapidly although I avoided publicity wherever possible as it often had strongly negative results from those who were unhappy at seeing increasing numbers of black people on the streets. My reputation certainly spread among the police forces and my services were sought not only by the local constabulary, but by neighbouring police in Paddington and Notting Hill who also called me out in the early hours of the morning to deal with developing situations resulting from the noise of parties. I would drive at speed through the empty streets some 4 or 5 miles from my home in Craven Park Harlesden to an address in Paddington, wondering what I would say if I were stopped by the police for speeding and thinking I should ask them to fit flashing lights on my car!

The vast damage caused by a severe hurricane that hit Jamaica in 1951 prompted many more people to seek the means for a passage to Britain. Women and children also began coming in increasing numbers. One of the outcomes of this change from predominantly male migrants was an increase in the number of young men seeking to get married. They were finding it hard to care for themselves alone and finding a wife who would share the household burdens became highly desirable.

A Multiracial Congregation

Monica and I moved from Harlesden to Tottenham in north London near the end of 1957, but our reputation went ahead of us and large numbers of Caribbean migrants began coming to our new church at High Cross in the centre of Tottenham opposite the Town Hall, where I became Mayor's Chaplain three times during the following 10 years.

By this time, I had published the book *Black and White in Harmony* and I was doing a regular weekly radio broadcast for the BBC on their Caribbean Service – *'A Letter from London'* – reporting on life in London among the migrant communities. I tried to give a realistic portrayal of the difficulties that many of them faced in issues such as accommodation and employment, hoping that this might stem the flow, thus giving us time to absorb the numbers coming into selective parts of London. But the political pressures for legislation to control immigration were growing and rumours abounded in the Caribbean that the days of unhindered entry into Britain were now numbered. This increased the flow of migrants to a peak in 1961 and in the next six months, before the Immigration Act came into effect in July 1962.

Our church in Tottenham was a much larger building than we had had at Harlesden and so too was the congregation. There were a few black worshippers when we arrived including a nurse from Trinidad, working at the nearby Prince of Wales Hospital. But the number of West Indians attending the church increased quite rapidly. In fact, our numbers often filled the 1000-seater church to capacity, with both white and black people sitting together in what was reported to be the largest multiracial congregation in Britain.

It was remarkable how a white congregation of some 500 absorbed a large number of black worshippers with great goodwill. There was very little friction and as far as I am aware, we only lost one couple who came into the church for the regular Sunday evening service and found some black people occupying their usual seat. They immediately turned around and walked out of the church and never came back. She was a lady of some social significance as a local magistrate, but her attitude and actions were not widely shared by the congregation, even when we encountered social problems on a wider scale.

In 1961 the BBC asked permission to broadcast our morning service on Commonwealth Sunday on its Caribbean Service where I was a regular presenter. Inevitably, this attracted a larger number than usual. People from the Caribbean came from all over London and although we relayed the service from the church, seating 1,000 into the church hall which seated a further 500, every seat was taken both in the church and in the hall and still there were several hundred people outside who could not gain entry. In the sermon I spoke about race relations in Britain; I was working on a television programme on mixed marriages which in those days were very rare and quite controversial. Some of the things I said were picked up by the national press which brought our church to the attention of those who strongly opposed immigration.

For several Sundays after the broadcast, members of the National Front picketed the church, handing out anti-immigration literature to people entering the church. The height of this disruption of our church life was reached when unknown assailants attacked the church house during the night throwing white paint over our front door and windows and painting insulting slogans on the pavement in front of the house – even using the hated 'N' word.

The reaction from the local population was remarkable. Far from joining in the criticism of the church and our ministry, small groups of local residents came to help clear up the damage to the house and remove slogans from the wooden fence at the side of the property. The Borough Council immediately sent workmen to clear up the slogans painted on the pavement. They were unable to clear away the paint, so they simply turned the paving stones upside down. As far as I am aware those slogans are still there today!

Caribbean Visit

It was a bitter experience for young hopefuls who came to the mother country full of high regard and expectation of a warm welcome. When I visited Barbados, Trinidad, and Jamaica in the early 1960s I spoke to many people of all ranks in society who were considering emigrating to Britain and who actually referred to it as 'going home'. The first time I heard this I made the mistake of asking where they had previously lived in Britain, to be regarded with astonishment, saying that this would be their first visit to the mother country, centre of the Empire.

Of course, before my visit to the West Indies, I had read a great deal about colonial history, the infamous Slave Trade Triangle between Africa, the Americas, and Britain, including the incredible cruelty of plantation slavery, so I fully expected a hostile reception. The reality was quite the reverse and time after time I found myself embarrassed by the warmth expressed towards everything British – especially as I knew that the warm expressions would not be reciprocated when they reached Britain.

In Jamaica I spoke at many churches in different parts of the island, both in towns and rural areas and everywhere I was given an almost embarrassing welcome with expressions of love towards Britain and recollections of English or Scottish teachers and ministers who had served them in their town or village. From them they had learned a glowing picture of life in Britain that increased their desire to emigrate and to share the good life and prosperity that they felt assured was awaiting them. I suppose their English teachers had spoken warmly about 'going home' and so they used the same expression for their own hopes.

In many conversations I raised the subject of slavery, but in almost every case there was a strong unwillingness to respond. I was often told bluntly that it was all in the past and was not a subject ever discussed in normal family life. But in so many different rural areas I saw existing the evidence of plantation slavery in the ruins of buildings including great houses that had been neglected for generations.

The evidence was everywhere on the island, but nobody wanted to talk about it. It was over and done with, and in many people, I sensed an embarrassment when I raised the subject. Of course, it may have been that I was a white man and an Englishman, and they were reluctant to express views that might offend me, although I tried to make it clear that I viewed the whole history of plantation slavery as abhorrent, and I deeply regretted the actions of my ancestors. There were, nevertheless, a few among the more socially aware people, with whom I was able to have some in-depth conversations on Jamaica's past history.

My experience of life in Barbados, Trinidad, and Jamaica was inevitably limited both by time and by the fact that I was a visitor from an entirely different culture. Even though I spent some months in Jamaica and quite literally travelled from one end of the island to the other and had the opportunity of meeting people in rural areas as well as in the towns, being a visitor is a very different experience from actually being born in the local culture.

In the next chapter my colleague and friend Alton Bell, who was born in Jamaica where he spent his early boyhood, shares his first-hand experience which gives a valuable insight into life on both sides of the Atlantic Ocean. We have very different backgrounds, but we also have a lot in common, each taking a great interest in a wide range of areas of social justice and sharing a commitment to the Christian faith. As well as chairing MJR, Alton is the minister of a London church (and I still have some pastoral responsibilities for a church in Kentish Town, an inner-city area of central London). Alton's experience provides an invaluable insight into the social and emotional processes of adjusting from rural Jamaica to inner-city London, and I am grateful to him for sharing his thoughts in the following chapter.

Chapter 3

COLOUR CONSCIOUSNESS IN THE CARIBBEAN: THE JAMAICAN EXPERIENCE

In this chapter the Revd Alton P. Bell, minister of a London Church and chair of the Movement for Justice and Reconciliation (MJR), describes his life as a boy born in a rural village in Jamaica before the emigration of his father to England. He describes his father's experiences as a member of the Windrush Generation and his own great desire to follow him. He speaks about life as a schoolboy in London and his later experience in further education and employment. It gives a fascinating insight into life in the migrant community in Britain in the early days of the settlement.

Living in Jamaica

The island of Jamaica in the West Indies is divided into three counties and fourteen parishes. I was born in 1958 in the parish of St Catherine. This was 120 years after the enactment by the British UK Parliament of the abolition of the enslavement of Africans in the British Caribbean islands and territories. The Act was passed into law in 1833, but it was not implemented until 1st August 1838, which ended the five-year period of apprenticeship for the Africans.

As mentioned in Chapter One, some £20 million was paid to the owners of slaves by way of compensation, but nothing at all was paid to the Africans in compensation for their loss of freedom, their enforced transportation to the Caribbean and the incredible cruelty that they and their forebears had suffered over the past 300 years.

When the Africans were set free in Jamaica no help of any kind was given to them in terms of stimulating local industries, or the provision of social organisation, community development or education. The former slaves were simply set free to find their own employment, housing and provision and to survive in any way possible. Consequently, during the next 120 years until my birth very little industrialisation or economic prosperity had been achieved.

Village Life

In the village where I lived there was considerable poverty and hardship with everyone struggling to make a living in whatever way they could. My parents were working class folks, my mother was a housewife who looked after the family whilst my father worked at his trade as a tailor, making clothes for those in the locality whilst also cultivating the land on which he was born, to support his growing family. He was born in 1924 between the first and second World Wars.

When the second World War was over in 1945, America sought permission from the UK Government to recruit workers from the British colonies to harvest crops on their farms, particularly in the New England regions. The UK duly agreed and thus began a chapter in my father's life that would change the entire history of the Bell family.

My Father's Emigration

At the tender age of 22 years my father, Allan Bell, along with a string of young Jamaican men, left the Island, many for the first time of leaving the island, to travel to the United States on a tour of six months, to harvest fruits, vegetables, sugarcane, grain, and anything else that was designated to them. This engendered in him the passion for travel and led to several tours of America during the late 1940s and 50s until he finally migrated to Britain. He arrived in England, the 'mother country', in 1961 and settled in north-west London where some of his cousins lived. He secured a job in a pharmaceutical factory in Perivale, Greenford, making tablets. He worked in the factory for almost 30 years until he retired and decided to move back to Jamaica permanently in the early 1990s.

The first five of Allan's children were born in Jamaica as British citizens. The pattern of our birth and the time span between us reflects our father's travels to do farm work. When he decided to make the permanent move to England, he worked day and night to save enough money to send for his family. First, he sent for our mother Myrtle in 1962 and soon after her arrival she fell pregnant and gave birth to our youngest brother in August 1963.

First House

During this period, my parents were living in rented accommodation. A year after the birth of our brother, mum and dad sent for our oldest sibling who lived with them in their rented accommodation. After moving to and from different locations, Allan decided to acquire a mortgage and buy a house for his family to live in. Our first house was, in Harlesden, north-west London. This was a five-bedroom semi-detached town house, and to help to pay the mortgage, he rented out a few rooms.

In 1967 my father sent for his youngest sibling, securing a job for him at the factory where he worked and gave him accommodation at his home in Harlesden. I was nine at the time, living with our grandparents in Point Hill, St Catherine, Jamaica. We were encouraged to correspond with our parents regularly. And they in turn would send provisions as parcels, or money, every month for our upkeep and for our education. In those days, every child had to pay for their education.

Moving to England

I was particularly incensed that our father had sent for our uncle rather than myself and my older brother. Consequently, at the tender age of nine I wrote him a very terse letter expressing my dismay at his decision. This led to the promise that he would send for us the next year. And so, in May 1968 my older brother and I boarded the BOAC airplane for the first time at Norman Manley airport in Kingston and travelled to England via Canada to join our parents.

At this point in my life, I had no idea of the struggles my parents had lived through in the decade of the sixties. I was totally oblivious to the issues of racism and how difficult it had been to acquire suitable accommodation in those days. I later learned that when our parents went to rent rooms, they were met with notices in the corner shops that stated: 'No Coloured, no Irish and no dogs.'

In the Caribbean our educational system was based on merit and ability. If you had the ability, then the teachers would ensure that you were entered for the relevant scholarship to get to high school. And if you had older siblings, then they also would coach you so that you passed the relevant entrance exam. In the UK, particularly in the area in north-west London where we lived, the Inner London

Education Authority had brought in the Comprehensive Education system, where everyone was treated the same, irrespective of their ability.

School Experience

I went to the local primary school at the bottom of our road and my older brother was sent to a local comprehensive school about two miles from our home in Harlesden. He ended up being put into classes doing work that he had completed several years before in Jamaica, which was boring for him, so he did not enjoy school.

Whilst living in Jamaica all our teachers looked and spoke like us. In England everything was different. All the teachers were white and none of them spoke like us. We were the minority in our classes, and this would have significant consequences, as I will explain later. At primary school I played in the cricket team and enjoyed some good success. Cricket was the national sport in Jamaica and every young boy aspired to be a cricketer. When the West Indies cricket team was playing, we would all gather around anyone who had a transistor radio to listen.

Secondary School

The transition from primary school to secondary school was seamless and uneventful. Back in Jamaica to transition you would have to take the equivalent of the eleven plus exam and could get a scholarship if you performed well in the exam. All of my older siblings achieved passes in this exam and were either given a full scholarship or a half scholarship to attend high school.

The state schools in the London Borough of Brent had no such scheme, so transitioning was relatively easy. The shock for me would come as I progressed through the school. Willesden High School was a typical comprehensive school. It used to be the Willesden County Grammar school until 1966 when it was transitioned to a comprehensive. We were placed into classes according to our surname. My surname being Bell, I was placed in 1A along with all those children having surnames beginning with A, B and C.

There were quite a number of black children in the school at this time. Many shared similar stories to me. Their parents had migrated from Jamaica in the early sixties and then subsequently sent for them. All of us lived in the Harlesden, Neasden, Willesden, Kensal Green and Kensal Rise areas and many of our parents worked in factories in Park Royal, on the buses leaving from Willesden Bus garage, and on the trains parked in the sidings at Willesden Junction station. London Transport and the surrounding local hospitals, Central Middlesex and the newly built Northwick Park Hospital serving Brent and Harrow, were major employers for our parents' generation. As stated earlier, my father worked at a pharmaceutical factory in Perivale and my mum worked part-time, usually on the night shifts at McVitie's biscuit factory in Waxlow Road, Harlesden.

Growing up was fun and playing sports on Saturday morning for the school was particularly exciting. It was exciting as we travelled to different areas to play against other local schools. The only drawback for me was when we had to play football in the driving rain, or on a snow-laden pitch which was often freezing. As I progressed through the school, I can remember hearing older boys lamenting the fact that they were excluded from playing professional sports for several of the local professional teams because of the colour of their skin. What became evident over time was that the vast majority of black boys were generally very good at sports, and this would take precedence over their academic pursuits.

During this period in the history of schooling in England, the education authorities had a two-tier exam system. Ordinary level qualifications would allow you to go on to doing subjects at advanced level which would lead to university admission; and Certificate of Secondary Education with its top mark equivalent to a grade 'C' in 'O' Level. Astonishingly, the vast majority of black children were placed in the CSE stream. It was as if we were being educated to fill the incessant need for trades people. Luckily, I had a young vibrant chemistry teacher who believed in me and after completing my CSE Chemistry exam I did my O level exam within six months and went on to join the A level class midway through the year. Needless to say, I went on to work for a precious metals chemical processing plant in North Acton, west London and they duly paid my fees to study chemistry at Higher National Certificate and then at degree level.

College Life

Whilst studying at college and then at a Polytechnic, it became quite glaring that as a black man I was always in the minority in my class. At college, the only other black person in my class was a middle-aged man of African origin, who was obviously struggling to keep up. Once I joined the degree stream, there were two black people in my class, one an African overseas student and the other a young man of Jamaican origin who lived in Slough. I did not engage much with the African overseas students, but I struck up a friendship with the Jamaican man that is still on-going after 40 plus years.

The school I attended was fairly mixed; the sports teams were fully mixed, the athletics squads were mixed; even the Christmas productions were mixed. Leaving school and going straight into the workplace was another education in itself. After obtaining a job as a trainee at that processing plant in North Acton, I was advised and helped to find alternative employment as there was a possibility of my developing 'Platinum Asthma'.

Factory Work

Although it was a long shot, the Company did not want to be faced with any litigation, so they actively helped me to get another job, having paid for my studies. Whilst seeking other employment, it started to dawn on me that I was the in the minority in my chosen profession. I was the only black person working in the laboratory at a site in North West London where over 2000 people were employed. The majority of the workforce in the factory making automobile instruments were black, with a small proportion of Asian and Irish folk. This pattern of having only a few black professionals in the workforce in North-West London was common throughout the UK. This was really the next step in my racial awareness, and I found myself asking the question:

Why is there a disparity between educational outcome and the colour of an individual's skin?

The socio-economic realities of growing up in an urban area with the pressure to make ends meet dictated that as each member of the family came of age they were expected to help in the upkeep and running of the household. This was no different for my family and

35

after completing my elementary studies it was now my turn to find gainful employment. This I duly did and also embarked on further studies on a day-release scheme.

More Training

The day-release scheme meant that you worked for four days and went to college/university for one full day to pursue higher qualifications. It seemed that the economic, and social construct dictated how certain groups behaved and if you were part of that group, society knew what to expect from you. This method of operation would become more apparent to me as my understanding grew about the construction of Caribbean society back in the 18th and 19th centuries.

Whilst working at Smith Industries in Cricklewood London, with its diverse workforce, I encountered the vagaries of the world of work. As a professional industrial chemist, I worked in the laboratories, developing anti-freeze, testing materials, and analysing solutions. I was introduced to a plethora of different people and a rigid class system. I enjoyed mixing with the wide variety of people, Asians, Anglo-Asians, Irish, English, people from different West-Indian Islands and so on.

Social Differentiation

This was the early 80s and the workforce reflected society at large. What was very apparent though, was the rigid demarcation that existed between the professional and working classes. Because I worked in the lab, I could eat in the ordinary canteen where the majority of the workforce ate; but I was also entitled to eat in the managers' canteen. However, I could not eat in the directors' canteen where only senior managers and directors ate. Needless to say, the level and presentation of the food increased as you went from workers' to directors' canteens.

The company had a variety of in-house teams, including a football team, a cricket team, golf team and indoor-games teams. They also had a fire brigade which competed against other branches in other parts of the country. I played in the cricket and football teams and also joined the fire brigade. This gave me the opportunity to mingle with members from the general workforce, meeting people from all parts of the company and also from different strata of society.

Friendships

One particular person who became a very good friend was a young English man who worked on the shop floor and was a Union rep. It turned out that he came from Yorkshire and was a graduate of Cambridge University. As I got to know him, it transpired that he was a socialist who agitated for workers' rights and took ordinary jobs to identify with the ordinary workers. He later went into teaching and ended up marrying a Caribbean woman from Grenada.

During my six years working for Smith's Industries my life took a dramatic turn. Because I had to liaise with people who worked in different areas, I regularly met up with Peter who worked in the cliché shop. Here he made screens to print the facias for the instrument dials. We were developing flexible plastic conductors rather than the rigid circuit boards that were being used.

Marriage and Homemaking

Peter taught me the process of screen printing and introduced me to golf. He lived in Luton, and it was in conversation with him that I bought my first house. He expressed to me that he had a second house that he wanted to sell and asked if I was interested. I spoke with my father about it and he said, 'Why not?' He provided the deposit for me, and I bought my first house at the age of 21. This was life-changing since after fixing up the house and renting it for a few years, I was later destined to meet my wife and life partner who shared this house with me after we married in 1983.

A year after my marriage, Smith's Industries closed the factory in Cricklewood and made us redundant. I took a job at Luton College of Higher Education as a laboratory technician although I was over-qualified for the job. However, as a young married man who was now a Christian, this turned out to be another seminal life-changing moment.

Life in Sri Lanka

I now lived and worked in Luton. Whilst working at the college, the head of the science department, Dr Jo Duoek, invited me to be part of a team she was assembling to take on a training exercise in Sri Lanka. I jumped at the opportunity and for three weeks in the summer I and my colleagues visited the British Council and various educational institutes teaching, in my case how to maintain their analytical instrumentation. The programme went on for three years even though I left the job after 19 months.

During my visits to various parts of Sri Lanka, I saw the brutal impact of colonialism. The tea plantations were usually sited on hills; however, the planters were usually generations of families, who were born on the plantations, lived and worked on the plantations and died on the same plantations. This resonated with the lifestyles of those people who were born on the plantations in the Caribbean Islands.

Social Awareness

At this stage of my understanding of social awareness, I knew very little about the history or the plight of colonised people. The disregard for the humanity of the people who lived and worked on the tea plantations brought tears to my eyes, especially on returning home when I reflected on the images of smiling tea pickers on the side of red buses driving around the streets of London.

After leaving Luton College of Higher Education, I took a job in the Industrial Chemistry Department at City University, London. I was now working at the heart of academia, and with the professor and other staff members of the department, I embarked on research to alleviate the problems of using domestic gas boilers in hard water areas.

During this period of my life, I was still involved with the British Council project in Sri Lanka and I was very active in my local church in North-West London that my mother had started. The Sri Lanka project lasted for three years. As technologists, scientists, and engineers, we were paid an honorarium, and our business class air fares and stays in five-star hotels were paid for in full.

Visiting Jamaica

After I qualified as a chemist, and prior to visiting Sri Lanka, I had visited Jamaica with my sister who had lived there until she was a teenager. She alerted me to the fact that up until the 1970s, all the workers in the banks and public-facing businesses were light skinned. There was a conscious effort to maintain this colonial status. As I visited the tea plantations and the various institutes in Sri Lanka, it suddenly occurred to me that the majority of those who worked on the plantation were dark-skinned whilst those who were public-facing and worked in the hotels were of a lighter hue. Sri Lanka was a mirror image of Jamaica. The state of the roads, the methods of travel for the majority of people and the hierarchical pigmentocratic system, were all part of the British colonial legacy.

I was now on a trajectory to help to alleviate this situation and address the sense of injustice that I felt for marginalised people. As a Christian, I was taught that all human beings were made in the image of God. However, it was baffling to me why those who had a darker skin tone were treated differently irrespective of where they lived in the world. This started my quest to gain knowledge and understanding of how this system of pigmentation came about – what were its origins and how it can be dismantled?

Chapter 4

INTEGRATION

This chapter leaves Alton Bell's personal reflections of life in London as a young immigrant and moves to a consideration of the social issues that confronted the community of which he was a member. As a contrast, this chapter looks at the same issues, but from outside the immigrant community. Clifford Hill notes the formation and growth of the first of the African Caribbean churches in Britain, the New Testament Church of God, that provided a sanctuary for both Pentecostals and non-Pentecostal immigrants in the early days of their settlement in Britain, and explores the possibility of this being a response to status deprivation.

Community Problems

One of the problems facing the first generation of migrants from the West Indies was their limited knowledge of the situation in Britain that they would encounter. The English people with whom they came into contact in their native Isles were usually of the executive or professional classes such as teachers, clergy, or colonial officials. Before coming to Britain none of the migrants had any experience of, or contact with, the English working classes. The majority of the newcomers settled in the depressed inner-city areas of London where people were already struggling with a range of social problems and where there was an acute shortage of housing due to the vast number of houses that had suffered bomb damage during the war and had not yet been repaired or replaced.

The people who were now their closest neighbours were often those who had not had the initiative or the means to move out to the suburbs, or those who had been embittered by the unequal struggle to cope with poverty and unemployment. When they saw their coloured neighbours buying houses in their street and filling them with their friends there was considerable resentment. They had no understanding of the way the West Indians achieved this through their self-help schemes. They did not know that a number of the migrants would agree to form a savings group with one of them acting as treasurer to collect weekly instalments. They would then take it in turn to receive the whole amount collected that week, which gave the recipient sufficient money to lay down the deposit for a mortgage on a house. This would enable him to offer accommodation to others and to receive rental income to meet his mortgage repayments, as well as to house his own family. This was the way many of them became home-owners.

Home Ownership

Many of the social tensions in the inner-city areas of London in the 1950s were caused by overcrowding and the lack of basic facilities. It was a time of great injustice and exploitation of the most vulnerable by ruthless profiteering landlords such as Rachman, whose name became synonymous with profiteering from rundown and overcrowded houses rented to people who had desperate needs and no alternatives. When black landlords were seen to be property owners they were immediately associated in the public mind with such exploitation even if their motives were those of community service rather than exploitation. But the social gap between black and white residents was such that there was very little interracial communication. So, neither group got to know each other. Tensions grew over minor issues and when they reached a certain pitch they would boil over into open conflict as happened with the Notting Hill riots in 1958.

Lack of Advice

One of the things I found most frustrating was the lack of any official help being given to the immigrants from what in those days was called the 'New Commonwealth'.[8] An old wartime underground shelter underneath Clapham Common was opened to give emergency temporary accommodation to the first migrants who came on the 'Empire Windrush' in 1948 as they had nowhere to go in London. But although their numbers continued to increase steadily during the next four or five years there was no government action to provide help or advice for them, other than the regular Citizens

---

8   This term was largely used to distinguish between black and white immigrants: i.e. between those coming from the West Indies, Africa, India and Pakistan; and those coming from Australia and Canada.

Advice Bureaux. In fact, the Home Office did not even bother to count the number of immigrants coming into Britain until 1955, so no statistics are available for immigration before that year. It was not regarded as a Home Office issue until community tensions reported in the press forced it upon the attention of the Government.

Immigration Numbers

The following table gives a picture of the earliest years of immigration from New Commonwealth countries into the UK.

TABLE 1
Net immigration from the New Commonwealth into UK[9]

Year	West Indies	Pakistan	India	Others	TOTAL
1955	27,550	1,850	5,800	7,500	**42, 700**
1956	29,800	2.030	5.600	9,400	**46,850**
1957	23,000	5,200	6,600	7,600	**42,400**
1958	15,000	4,700	6,200	3,950	**29,850**
1959	16,400	850	2,950	1,400	**21,600**
1960	49,650	2,500	5,900	350	**57,700**
1961	66,300	25,100	23,750	21,250	**136,400**
1962a	31,800	25,080	19,050	18,970	**94,900**
1962b	3,241	137	3,050	2,531	**8,685**
1963	7,928	16,336	17,498	15,287	**57,049**
1964	14,848	10,980	15,413	20,776	**62,117**
1965	13,400	7,427	18,815	13,775	**53,417**
1966	9,620	8,008	18,402	10,923	**46,953**
1967	10,080	21,176	22,638	10,713	**64,637**
1968	4,801	14,876	28,340	18,686	**66,703**

a Jan 1 - June 30   b July 1 - Dec 31

It is interesting to see that in 1955 whereas there were 27,550 migrants from the West Indies, there were only 1,850 from Pakistan and 5,800 from India. That pattern remained for the next two years and then the whole pattern of migration began to change towards the end of the decade as the post-war employment boom disappeared and tales of hardship from the migrants were being well publicised in their home countries. There were fewer people keen to come to Britain to endure the experience of those who were already here.

9 Reproduced from Clifford Hill, *Immigration and Integration, A Study of the Settlement of Coloured Minorities in Britain*, Pergamon Press, Oxford 1970, 27. Original source: Home Office statistics.

Notting Hill Riots

The big game-changer, however, was undoubtedly the Notting Hill riots in September 1958 which caused an immediate drop in immigration, not just from the West Indies, but also from India and Pakistan where the following year only 850 came from Pakistan and 2,950 from India. Another major change came in 1960 when immigration became a political matter. The riots had forced the whole subject of immigration to the forefront of the nation. Newspapers had been full of dramatic accounts and pictures of turmoil and destruction. The social pressures and tensions in the inner-city areas where migrants were settling forced a range of social issues onto the political agenda. These issues were not just about the numbers of immigrants, but about housing, education, health and welfare.

Pressures mounted for the introduction of curbs on immigration, and this had an immediate effect overseas as well as in Britain. The political debates were published in the newspapers in all the West Indian islands as well as in India and Pakistan. This immediately raised alarm among those who had relatives already in Britain and had hopes of joining them. The fear of not being able to get into Britain spread widely across New Commonwealth countries and this was immediately reflected in the figures for immigration in 1960 as seen in the above table. West Indian immigration leapt from 16,000 in 1959 to nearly 50,000 in 1960.

India and Pakistan

There was a similar leap in immigration from India and Pakistan and it was this that caused alarm in Britain and was voiced in Westminster. The intention to introduce limits on immigration caused numbers to skyrocket during 1961, with more than 66,000 coming from the West Indies, 25,000 from Pakistan and nearly 24,000 from India. It was the migration from India and Pakistan with their immense populations that caused alarm bells to ring loudly in Westminster. The Commonwealth Immigrants Act 1962 was passed following acrimonious debate and a vast amount of coverage in newspapers and radio and TV debates. It came into force in July 1962, but the figures for the first six months of 1962 show the extent of the rush to reach Britain before the limits were imposed.

All these debates in Parliament triggered a vast amount of public debate on the wide range of social issues related to immigration. Collectively, the national debate had the effect of generating the concept that the presence of coloured people in Britain was a social problem. Throughout the 1950s the migrants were mainly from the Caribbean islands where English was their first language and both their legal and educational systems were based upon British law and custom. But 1961 saw large numbers coming into Britain from India and Pakistan, most of whom could not speak English and who were from other religions with very different social customs and values which began rapidly to change the whole character of the migrant population and put additional strain upon health and welfare services.

Caribbean Christian Cultures

By contrast, the immigrants from the Caribbean islands came from strongly Christian cultures with some 75% of the population in regular church attendance. It is very revealing to note that 70% of this church attendance was in churches of the same denominations as we have in Britain – the Roman Catholic, the Church of England, the Methodist, the Baptist, the Congregational, and the Presbyterian Churches. A further 5% attended churches of Pentecostal sects.

Christianity was their national religion and in theory they should have been able to integrate easily into British society. However, as we have already noted, a 1963 survey showed that only 4% of West Indian migrants were attending churches in the London area. There were many reasons for this large decline in church attendance which include social factors such as some of them having to work on Sundays, but the outstanding reason has to be the fact that they did not feel welcome in the same denominational churches where they had worshipped in their home islands.

Pentecostal Groups

This disaffection from the main Christian denominations is further underlined by the rapid growth of West Indian led Pentecostal groups that have grown into large church organisations – like the New Testament Church of God in the early years of the migration period.

TABLE 2[10]
The New Testament Church of God in England

	1966	1968	1970
Administrative Districts	10	12	15
Full-time Ministers	15	20	24
Owned Premises	17	24	29
Rented Premises	44	45	45
Congregations	62	69	74
Baptised Membership	2,500	3,300	3,600
Adherents in Regular Attendance	3,600	7,000	10,000
Children and Young People	4,400	5,500	7,000
Total Sect Membership	10,500	15,800	20,600

The New Testament Church of God is the oldest of the churches established by migrants from the West Indies in Britain. It was founded by the Revd Oliver Lyseight in 1952 which was the same year as I began ministry in London, and we became firm friends. Initially I was not at all happy with his attempts to find premises to start his own group in the Hammersmith area of London. I both spoke and wrote against the formation of separate immigrant congregations. I warned that this could develop into a 'religious apartheid' in Britain with separate white and black churches which would be similar to the situation in South Africa.

Formation of NTCG

Oliver Lyseight told me that he and his fellow Pentecostal friends had attended many churches including Pentecostal Assemblies in England, and in none of them did they feel welcome. This was the reason why he started with a small group which rapidly grew in London, so then he started a similar one in Birmingham. By the end of the 1950s the number of groups was growing in inner-city areas across Britain.

In the face of all the evidence of the difficulties West Indian Christians were finding in integrating into the churches in Britain, and also taking into account the changing social situation following

---

10   Clifford Hill, 'Immigrant Sect Development in Britain: A Case of Status Deprivation?' in *Social Compass* XVIII, 1971/2, 232. *Social Compass* was an academic journal of sociology, and the use of the word 'sect' in this context is a sociological term for a group that is not part of a main denomination.

the Notting Hill riots, I had to rethink the stand I had taken against the formation of separate congregations. I nevertheless expressed the hope that this would be a transitional measure and that in due time, having established flourishing congregations and thereby demonstrating their leadership ability, the separate black-led churches would come together with the traditional white churches in Britain to form fully mixed congregations.

The membership of the NTCG doubled in the four years 1966 to 1970, jumping from a membership of 10,500 to 20,600. In 1966 they had 61 congregations, mainly in Birmingham and London, but they also had 15 full-time ministers and a theological college training 20 students for the ministry. My wife, Monica, was actively involved in teaching at their college at Overstone in Northamptonshire. She took an active share in formulating their training programme for ministers and giving advice on the establishment of the college as an academic institution.

FIGURE 1
Growth Pattern of the New Testament Church of God: 1950 to 1970 [11]

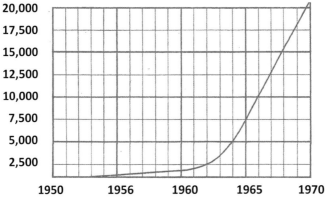

Total membership including adherents in regular attendance

Links with Race Relations

Their national headquarters was in Birmingham, but they had already spread to 8 provinces across the country each with a full-time 'Overseer.' It is revealing to note the growth pattern of the New

11 Taken from Clifford Hill, *Black Churches: West Indian and African sects in Britain*, Community and Race Relations Unit of the British Council of Churches, London 1971, 17.

Testament Church of God which shows a clear correlation between the rise in membership and the deterioration of race relations in Britain. This is shown in the graph on the last page.

The growth pattern of the NTCG was very slow during the early 1950s. Rapid growth began soon after the Notting Hill riots of 1958, and the growth pattern accelerated from 1960 when immigration became a major issue of national debate. The next hike in the growth rate occurred in 1964 with the General Election when race relations became a major issue with the electorate. The election was won by Labour, but just one seat went against the national trend. It was won by Peter Griffiths MP for Smethwick who wrote to his constituents warning that the birth rate of the local Asian migrants was eight times higher than that of the white population.

This gave a birth rate of 122 per thousand which was, of course, nonsense since the national rate in India at that time was only 40 per thousand. What Griffiths failed to note was that practically all the Asian immigrants were in the childbearing age which could not be compared with the whole population of Britain or of India.

Relative Deprivation

In an article published in the academic sociological journal *Social Compass,* on the subject of immigrant churches in Britain, I said that:

> In terms of relative deprivation and its underlying basis in reference group theory, the comparative reference group of first-generation immigrants is usually found in their home societies. As these groups are usually deprived, either economically or in terms of some other significant variable, a high level of dissatisfaction among such immigrants is not normally found.

New Commonwealth immigrants to Britain are, however, experiencing both ethnic and status deprivation. This is particularly true of the light brown and fair skinned West Indian who has high status in the Caribbean colour graded system of social differentiation, but who are simply classed as 'coloured' in Britain. No distinction is made by the British between black and fair coloured – all are low status. The black man has been used to being low status, but for the fair skinned coloured man it is a new experience.[12]

---

12   Hill, 'Immigrant Sect Development in Britain', 234.

Colour Differentiation

It took me a long time to understand this form of colour differentiation. When we moved from Harlesden to our second church in Tottenham, north London, there was a fair-skinned young lady in the choir. She was a nurse from the local hospital who originally came from Trinidad. She was the only coloured person in the choir, and she was clearly a favourite with the others who were all white English people. She no doubt enjoyed the special attention that she received. But soon after our arrival significant numbers of West Indians began moving into the area and attending our Sunday evening congregation.

Most of these newcomers were from Jamaica and on numerous occasions the young nurse spoke critically of them. I assumed that this was some form of inter-island rivalry because I was not aware of the existence of a colour code, even though I had been working among the Caribbean migrants for the past five years. I was, of course, aware that some were black, and others were brown. But I had no awareness of colour code differentiation. The young lady from Trinidad had very fair skin and most of the newcomers from Jamaica were either black or brown. It was not until I visited the West Indies in 1961 that I realised the significance of the deprivation experienced by migrants of light skin when we treated everyone with the same honour. The young nurse no doubt felt that her high status was being threatened by the newcomers who were mostly of a darker colour, but they were being accorded the same welcome as she had been enjoying. Her own social status within the church community was therefore being threatened.

Deprivation

Deprivation has the effect of driving together, in social solidarity, members of a minority group. Thus, the rapid rise in membership of black-led immigrant churches is, arguably, a response to the experience of social deprivation, as we see illustrated in Figure 1 above. Observers of the British race relations scene trace the beginnings of the hardening of racial attitudes to 1964, the year of the General Election where, for the first-time, race and immigration became major issues. The growth pattern of the NTCG reflects this, although there are two other variables that need to be evaluated before we can affirm this correlation.

The first variable is gender. In Jamaica roughly 70% of the New Testament Church of God members in the 1960s were women.[13] This compared with a 60/40% ratio in Britain at that time. Home Office immigration figures showed that from 1958 the proportion of female to male immigrants rose significantly; from this we would expect the proportion of women members of the NTCG to increase, particularly as the majority of migrants were coming from rural areas in Jamaica where Pentecostals were strongest. But the male members of the church in Britain had begun attending earlier than this. So, we may conclude that the socially significant factor in this early male membership is linked with the deterioration in race relationships in Britain and the resultant rise in felt deprivation due to ethnic prejudice in the white population.

Male Social Status

Another factor that is worth noting is this; the West Indian male immigrant suffers a higher degree of loss of personal status than the female. Most women's occupations in working class West Indian society are confined to a fairly narrow range of domestic skills which are generally very poorly rewarded. Any industrial employment they obtain in Britain represents a relative rise in status. The men, on the other hand, except those from purely peasant farming backgrounds, are more likely to suffer a loss of status due to the lower evaluation of their skills in Britain.

The West Indian male also suffers a considerable degree of role uncertainty due to the change from the norm of common law marriage in the West Indies to that of legal marriage in Britain. Traditionally the legally married man is regarded as a patriarchal figure, but most West Indian women are better fitted for family leadership roles in terms of the traditions of social organisation and culture in which they have been reared.

The West Indian population is largely matriarchal which stems from the days of slavery when the older women who were no longer fit for field gang work were employed to take care of

---

13   This figure has been taken from sources quoted by M.J.C. Calley, in *God's People: West Indian Pentecostal Sects in England*, London 1965.

the children so that their mothers could work in the fields. The tradition of children being reared by their grandparents remains to this day; and inheritance of land usually passes down through the female line. Thus, in terms of relative deprivation, the West Indian male's loss of status rankings is the more severe. If we are right in linking Pentecostal church membership with the experience of felt deprivation, then we would expect to find a proportionately higher percentage of male members in Britain than in the West Indies. This is, in fact, demonstrated from the statistics in Figure 1.

Correlation

When we take into account the year that the growth of membership of these congregations began to rise sharply, we can see the correlation with the deterioration of race relations in Britain from the time of the 1958 Notting Hill riots. From 1964 the growth rate again rose sharply which also coincided with the whole subject of race relations becoming politicised. We may therefore conclude with some confidence that there was a definite correlation between this growth and the experience of status deprivation due to ethnic prejudice. The compensatory functions of church membership for those suffering from status deprivation in wider society are well-known and need not be elaborated here.[14]

In 1971, in *Black Churches,* I wrote:

It would seem that there is a definite link between the experience of deprivation due to ethnic prejudice, and membership of the all-black immigrant churches in Britain. On this basis we may expect that so long as race relations in Britain continue to deteriorate, their membership will continue to increase. Whether or not this will hold true for the second-generation only time will tell.[15]

---

14   The literature back in the 1960s on the function of religion in relation to social and economic forces is extensive: e.g. M.G. Smith *et al.*, *The Ras Tafari Movement,* Institute of social and Economic Research, University College of the West Indies, 1960. O Patterson, 'Ras Tafari: the Cult of Outcasts', in *New Society*, 12 November 1964. A Kiev, 'Psychotherapeutic Aspects of Pentecostals among West Indian Immigrants to England', *British Journal of Sociology*, March 1964. B.R. Wilson, 'A Typology of Sects', in R. Robertson (ed.), *Sociology of Religion*, Penguin, London 1969.

15   Hill, 'Immigrant Sect Development', 19..

Fifty Years Later

It is some 50 years ago since I wrote those words during which time the New Testament Church of God has become established in the church scene in Britain having made great strides in their development. They are undoubtedly a well organised church with good leadership and a national presence. Looking back today, all these years later, we can say that there has been a great deal of progress in the formation of this church, and it has a proud history of serving large numbers of people of Caribbean ancestry in Britain.

There has, nevertheless, been a fall off in membership of the New Testament Church of God in recent years. The first generation continued to grow for many years peaking in the 1990s, but since then there has been a gradual decline as the older members of the churches have died, but they have not been replaced in sufficient numbers by the next generation. As will be seen from Figure 1 there was a period of rapid growth in the five years between 1965 and 1970 when they reached a membership of 20,000. This growth rate was maintained for the next 10 years, but it was followed by slow decline. This decline was a mirror image of what was happening among the traditional churches in Britain with largely white congregations. The members failed to retain their second-generation who were clearly wanting integration into wider society in Britain.[16] That integration included adopting the social values of the white majority in the population who were deserting the churches in large numbers. They no doubt did not share the faith of their parents and they probably saw going to church as a hindrance to integration.

Membership Today

On their website in August 2020, they stated that their membership stood at 11,000 although they also claim some 30,000 adherents. They have made enormous strides in administration and in establishing congregations in towns and cities across Britain, as well as in the education and training for their pastors and leaders.

They have also been successful in acquiring church premises and they are served by some 300 accredited pastors. But they have not been successful in maintaining their early growth rate

---

16   The social situation facing the second generation of immigrants is dealt with in the penultimate chapter of this book.

especially among families and young people. This, of course, is in line with the experience of many traditional churches in the mainline denominations in Britain. Their decline follows the general pattern of churchgoing in Britain. In the mainline churches the most successful are the ones that have transformed their mission outreach, modernising their worship and their whole approach to mission. It remains to be seen whether or not the NTCG will do something similar to serve their ethnic community or whether the days of separate black and white churches in Britain are numbered.

Full Integration

The full integration of black and white Christians had always been my hope. That was against all the sociological forces of change in the early days of the migration in the 1950s and 60s. I was forced to accept the inevitability of separate black and white churches. But I always regarded this as an interim measure, demonstrating the fact that black leaders had the ability to offer leadership in the churches with equal success alongside white ministers, although their leadership skills were not being recognised in the mainline churches.

It was my hope that the black-led churches would be demonstrably successful, and that the day would come when they would be open to seek the means of working together – black-led and white-led churches seeking the re-evangelisation of Britain on a new basis of racial equality and acceptance of each other's traditions and skills and spiritual experience, which would be mightily blessed by the power of the Holy Spirit.

It is still my hope that that day will come! Maybe the days of change **will** come after the great shaking of the nation by the coronavirus pandemic that closed churches and forced Christian leaders to stop and reflect upon the spiritual state of the nation and the mission of the church. Maybe in the days following the pandemic there will come a time of basic change in attitudes on both sides of the colour divide in Britain. If this is accompanied by a spirit of repentance for the past and creative hope for the future my dream might be fulfilled in much the same way as Martin Luther King had a mountaintop experience that gave him hope for the future.

Chapter 5
THE THIRD GENERATION THEORY OF SOCIAL CHANGE

This is an important chapter offering a theoretical explanation of social change. It explores the experience of different generations in migrant communities from a theoretical sociological perspective. It notes significant differences between the first and second generations, particularly in their attitudes towards integration into the dominant culture of the 'host nation'. These findings are particularly important for understanding what is happening in inner-city areas of Britain and the sociocultural issues faced by people of African Caribbean descent.

Windrush Generation

The starting point of putting a sociological framework around what we have been observing in the migration of men, women, and children from the West Indian territories to Britain, is to note the different generational stages in the settlement.

The 'Third Generation Hypothesis' was developed by Will Herberg in 1960 in a study of white immigrants in the USA. It was later refined in a study in Detroit by Lazerwitz and Rowitz. In this chapter we are applying the theory to the community in Britain who have their origins in the Caribbean.

First Generation Migrants

The basic theory is that the First Generation Migrants (here we are speaking of worker-migrants rather than students) enter their country of adoption in order to improve their lifestyles through better work opportunities and better living conditions. They often send money home to support their families. But although they are physically living in an alien country their socio/cultural centre remains in the country of origin.

This first generation of migrants has a limited desire for integration and they tend to form ethnic groups who maintain their cultural traditions. They have limited social or political ambitions so there is often no strong drive to overcome language or cultural barriers. They are content to live and work in the society of their adopted choice, but they have no wish for integration into its culture. This reinforces the desire to remain within their ethnic group and not seek for social acceptance in wider society. This leads to a tendency towards ghettoisation which creates problems for the children of the first generation of migrants who, from the moment they enter nursery, playgroup, or school, enter a different culture and are forced to live in two worlds.

They find themselves living within the ethnic culture of their parents at home, but then they are also forced to live within the culture of the local children – their new peer group. The outcome is that these children are inadequately socialised by their parents in either the local culture, or in the ethnic culture. The result of this culture clash is the creation of a 'generation gap' between parents and children which widens with age. By the time the children reach adolescence they may be in serious rebellion against the parents' ethnic culture which creates a range of social problems for them within their peer group. But it also creates problems within the family, as the parents begin to feel that they are losing the love and loyalty of their children.

Second Generation Migrants

The second generation migrants, who are the first generation to be born in the country of adoption, have very different objectives from their parents. Their aim is for full integration in the peer group culture and to make themselves fully acceptable within their local peer group. Their parents' homeland is a myth rather than a reality: it is part of the ethnic group mythology from which they wish to escape, because they see it as a barrier to the achievement of their objectives of peer group acceptance. This creates tensions within the family, especially if the parents have a poor grasp of the local language and culture.

For the second generation, the present reality is the country of their birth, not the country that their parents left before migration. It is their ambition to achieve acceptability in their birth country rather than in the unreal world of their parents. All their ambitions in terms of education and employment are in the society into which they have been born. The ethnic group culture of their parents is often seen as a barrier to integration. For many second generation migrants this means rejecting the norms of their parents and adopting peer group norms which they see as essential to the achievement of their objectives. The reality is that few actually succeed in their socio-economic ambitions which leaves the majority disappointed. The outcome is often a collective 'anomie' that often characterises second generation migrants who struggle to live with two cultural identities.

Blocked Social Goals

This is where blocked social goals present a particularly poignant problem for second generation migrants who lack the security of belongingness in the culture of their parents, but who also additionally lack the confidence born of achievement within their adopted culture. This contributes to the high rate of social deviance in second generation migrants.

This does not, of course, mean that all second generation migrants form a counterculture that is in rebellion with the local culture. These young people, like all human beings, react to different situations in different ways according to a mixture of temperament, family background and the social situation that confronts them. At this stage it may be worth looking at the different ways in which human beings react to the experience of blocked social goals – of not being able to achieve their desired ambitions.

FIGURE 2
Reaction to Blocked Social Goals (and see p. 56)

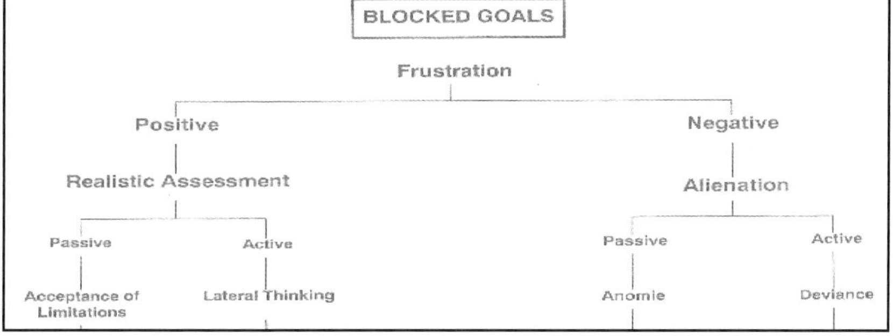

The negative and positive reactions to blocked social goals are well listed in the charts below. These have particular relevance for race relations as positive reaction enables individuals to overcome the disadvantage they may experience, whereas the negative reaction can lead to exacerbating disadvantage.

Positive Response to Blocked Social Goals

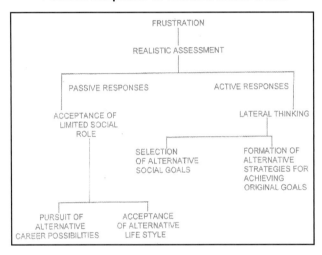

Negative Response to Blocked Social Goals

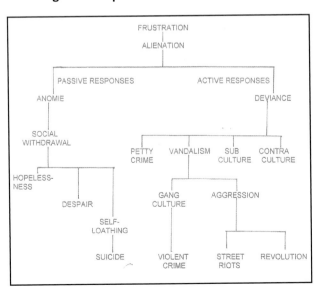

Third Generation Migrants

When we come to the third generation of migrants, their experience of life will be largely determined by living within the migrant community. If that community is living within confined geographical boundaries, their social and educational contacts will be limited. So too will they be limited in their first hand experience and their knowledge of the world outside the community.

They will, of course, have second hand knowledge of the world outside their immediate community through the media, especially through television and social media. But even in their education, their fellow students are likely to be of a similar background which can produce a shared culture of deprivation. In fact, there is statistical evidence showing that poor white communities experience greater educational disadvantage than black children living in the same neighbourhood.

Dangers

Such a culture leaves these young people highly vulnerable to exploitation from deviant operators (crooks!) who offer them easy money for delivering a package of drugs to someone in their community. Before long they are asked to look after a gun and keep it safe, or they find themselves drawn into a gang where members are expected to carry knives for personal defence in case of attack from rival gangs.

The objectives of the third generation migrants are very often determined by the experience of their parents. If their parents have achieved some measure of integration, their children will often react against the local culture and seek to discover a distinctive identity by searching for their roots in their grandparents' homeland.

This can go in one of two ways. If the individual achieves socio-economic security, he or she is happy to display their distinctive cultural identity while still playing a full part in the wider society. If, on the other hand, the individual is insecure, the tendency is to reject the peer group culture and look for security in traditional cultural groups, or local gangs, the outcome of which is alienation from wider society.

Theoretical Summary

The third generation theory states that the first generation of worker migrants are usually characterised by economic motives, but they lack the driving force of socio/political ambition, or the desire for social integration. They continue to identify with the culture and norms of their countries of origin.

The second generation seek full integration and therefore conform to the norms of the local peer group and reject the culture of their parents' ethnic group.

The third generation by contrast, if they are feeling secure in their peer group, will search for a distinctive identity in their family roots. They will actually find enjoyment in being different from the majority in wider society.

The theory was developed in America among white migrants and is only partially applicable to the British situation where ethnicity often makes it impossible for migrants of African or Caribbean origin to merge indistinguishably in white majority British society. This is where the whole subject of colour coding becomes particularly poignant, and this is why this chapter is included in this book where we are investigating the origins of prejudice that surrounds people with different degrees of colour.

The following examples show how this worked out in practice.

Caribbean Migrants from 1948

First Generation Migrants

With this theoretical background we will now look at the situation of the communities whose origins are in the West Indian islands and territories that were formerly part of the British Empire. As already mentioned in Chapter One, many of the first group of migrants who came on the 'Empire Windrush' in 1948 had served in the British Armed Forces during the Second World War. On demobilisation they returned to their home environment where economic prosperity was limited, and they decided to return to Britain where prospects were much more advantageous. Their objectives were similar to most first generation migrants in seeking better work and living conditions. They not only sent money home for family support, but also helped to pay the fare of another family member to come and join them.

The socio-cultural centre of the 'Windrush Generation' remained in their countries of origin but newly established ethnic groups, in particular West Indian-led churches, formed an important cultural centre and provided an expatriate support network. The migrants quickly adopted some of the norms of the local society particularly in terms of family and marriage. Throughout the 1950s and 60s thousands of young couples married and set up house together. This contrasted only in age with Caribbean culture where marriage was linked with socio-economic status and therefore was usually delayed until middle age, particularly in working class communities.

The immigrant couples were soon able to earn considerably more than they could in the Caribbean and marriage marked their new socio-economic status. But in their ethnic culture, family and marriage were part of a matriarchal culture in which the grandmothers care for the upbringing of the children. This was rooted in slavery where, on some plantations, marriage was forbidden to slaves under British colonial law until 1838.

The grandmother culture developed and became systemically embedded in the Caribbean culture after the abolition of the slave trade in 1807. This was due to further imports from West Africa becoming illegal and the only source of additional labour was through population expansion. The strongest male slaves were encouraged to have as many children as possible and the older women who were too weak for the field gangs became the child carers to the community. But in Britain there were no grandmothers, which put an inordinate strain upon the young mothers whose income was needed to meet the family budget and who struggled with the three roles – worker, mother, and wife. The result was a high rate of family breakdown and many children being inadequately socialised. The outcome was a severe generation gap between parents and children.

Second Generation Migrants

The objectives of the second generation migrants were full integration with the peer group in the local communities where they had been born and where they went to school. For many there was a problem of identity. They were black on the outside and white inside. Their parents still related to the culture of the Caribbean islands from which they had emigrated, but the culture, patois and mythology of the West Indies was alien to the children born in Britain.

They struggled with the two identities, and the desire for acceptance usually entailed rejection of the norms of their parents and the adoption of local peer group norms. For many of the second generation there was the additional struggle to attain educational qualifications in schools that were often part of the rundown inner-city environment where they grew up. It was an unequal struggle in which few succeeded in socio-economic terms. The outcome was a generation characterised by 'anomie', caused by a sense of rejection by wider society.

Third Generation Migrants

The third generation British African Caribbeans struggled to discover a distinctive identity. Many of them came from broken families with insecure parents who had produced dysfunctional family homes. They were unsure of their own identity and lacked a sense of purpose. Their parents were often unable to inspire them to achieve educational qualifications and gain social acceptance in the wider peer group culture. Their parents were also unable to provide them with a sound basis for personal and social morality since they had not been adequately socialised by their second generation parents.

This resulted in the formation of gangs as a substitute family. The gang provides identity, belongingness, security, protection, and comfort. Many third generation children reject the norms of what they see as a hostile society in which they cannot hope for social acceptance or economic achievement. The outcome is the formation of a counter-culture with its own 'in-group norms' and a form of alienation from wider society. Inevitably, in such a social group there will be a high rate of social deviance and a higher than average rate of legal offences and prison sentences. This, in turn, affects the attitudes of the legal enforcement authorities, police and probation services, who are more likely to suspect young people from black communities of being involved in crime, which affects 'stop and search' policies and results in a great many injustices and humiliations.

African Migrants from 1950s

It is interesting to apply third generation theory to African migrants in Britain because their communities, which rarely mix with the Caribbean communities (even in church!) provide some striking contrasts. But there is, in sociological terms, one major social variable between the two communities – colonial slavery, that applies only to Caribbeans. By isolating this variable we are enabled to draw some conclusions in regard to the legacy of slavery and its impact upon the West Indian migrant community in Britain.

The starting point requires a brief historical review which shows that the African migrants are approximately a whole generation behind the Caribbeans in terms of their settlement in Britain.

First Generation Migrants

Very few Africans came to Britain in the 1950s and 60s. Those who came were mainly from West Africa; from upper-class families who sent their children to Britain as students for advanced education. The objectives of these students were to gain educational qualifications and return to Africa. Most of them had no desire to settle in Britain and they returned to Africa where they formed a new educated professional middle-class elite often locally known as the 'Been Tos' – those who had 'been to' Europe for their further education. Many of these professional elite were disappointed with the social and political situation in Africa that they experienced upon their return home. This they compared with what they had observed in Britain which caused some of them to consider returning to settle in Britain.

From the 1980s onwards these Africans began to return to Britain in considerable numbers, or to send their children as first generation migrants. Their reference group cultural centre either remained in their original African communities or in the ethnic groups they created in Britain. African-led churches began to be formed in the 1990s and they soon became an important part of the expatriate community, providing opportunities to relax and enjoy congenial company free from the constraints of functioning in a society where acceptance is not guaranteed and in which cultural norms are not understood.

This first generation was mainly middle-class with leadership drawn from the professional classes. In the early days there was a high level of motivation, ambition, and entrepreneurship with strong desires for social acceptance and for the achievement of ambitions, using the education and skills they had already attained in Britain. Many of them married and established families in this country, and their ambitions for their children were even greater. There were strong motivations for economic improvement, but little desire for full social integration.

Many of this first generation of Africans had strong Christian convictions and were dismayed at the level of secularisation they saw in Britain. They longed to see spiritual revival and believed that God was calling them to live and work in Britain in order to help to create the conditions for revival. They eagerly joined all-night prayer meetings with twice yearly gatherings in excess of 40,000 in the Excel Centre in London since the year 2000 praying for revival in Britain. Those who had been educated in Britain understood the social environment and they had only limited concern for social acceptance into a culture they considered to be ungodly. Social friendships were mostly confined to relationships within the migrant communities or those encountered in the workplace.

Second Generation Migrants

The objective of the second generation – the first generation of Africans born in Britain – was for full integration with their local peer group. Many, however, were unsure of their identity, growing up in two cultures: the world of their parents which is part of the ethnic mythology from which they try to distance themselves in the transition from childhood to adolescence: and the world of school and local peer group norms which become increasingly important to them.

The African churches in Britain before the coronavirus pandemic in 2020 had the largest congregations of any other churches, either black or white. The numbers of children and young people attending these churches appear far larger than those attending black led Caribbean assemblies. It would appear that these churches, most of which have their origins in Nigeria, are more successful in holding their second generation than the Caribbean Pentecostal churches in Britain.

Like the second generation of Caribbean children, the African children also suffer the role conflict of being black on the outside and white inside. They know that if they are to achieve in socio-economic terms in wider society, they have to conform to the norms of that society. Many of them have parents who are highly ambitious for their children and put pressures upon them to succeed in obtaining educational qualifications which will lead to professional careers.

There are several factors that militate against educational attainment. These are:

- In a working-class area, the schools may not be of a particularly high standard.

- Local working-class norms will likely not encourage academic success.

- Black British culture has largely been formed by the Caribbean second and third generations whose counter-culture norms are contrary to academic success.

The outcome for many of these African young people is a struggle to find their identity in a clash of cultures. On the one hand there is the desire to please parents, or at least not to incur the wrath of parents, and on the other hand there is the desire for peer group acceptance.

In many ways their situation is more difficult than that of the Caribbeans', because their ethnic culture is patriarchal in contrast to the Caribbean matriarchal culture. There is a further differentiation in that the African culture is authoritarian rather than the liberal culture they experience in Britain. The pressures upon these young people can therefore often be intense, leading to depression or ill-health.

It is too early to assess the situation in regard to the third generation of Africans in Britain who have not yet been born.

Chapter 6
FAMILY AND MARRIAGE

This chapter describes a personal journey of discovery. It looks at the background of the 'Windrush Generation' at home in the West Indies through Clifford Hill's own observation in a 1962 visit. There is a description of attempts to discuss colonial slavery with people in Jamaica and observations on family, marriage, and concubine relationships. Some of these relationships are seen paralleled within the migrant communities in Britain where these same issues have links with the legacy of colonial slavery.

First Encounter

I can still remember the sense of shock I had when the first Caribbean couple came to me asking for a wedding which I described in Chapter One. It was 1952; I was fresh out of college, newly ordained in my first church with absolutely no experience of inner-city life and never having spoken to a black person in my life. I knew nothing about their background and nothing about the colonial history of the Caribbean islands and territories which were still British dependencies at that time. It would be another 10 years before Jamaica gained independence, and at that time all those in the British Caribbean territories were British citizens with a right to come to 'the motherland', the head of the British Empire.

My Caribbean journey of discovery began with one of the first couples requesting a wedding. I experienced a mild sense of surprise when I asked each of them where they lived, and they each gave the same address. This was the 1950s of the socially conservative post-World War II period. There was a great desire to return to some form of normality in home life with an emphasis upon traditional morality. Sexual morals were strictly observed in all social classes, especially in respectable working-class families.

Moral Mores

In my experience bride and groom did not live together in the same household until they were duly married. I took all the details, but then the real shock came when they said, "But while we are here, Parson, we would like to book the christening." In my naïveté I stupidly remarked that it was surely a bit premature to anticipate the happy event. They immediately said, "Well he's three months old and we'd like to get him done as soon as possible." In my middle-class world of social mores, it was unheard-of to have an illegitimate child and then to come and ask for a church wedding, with all the trimmings – a white gown, bridesmaids, with solemn vows and promises of fidelity.

My academic biblical theology fell apart at that moment and my real education began. I realised how little I knew and how much I had yet to learn if I were really to care for the people among whom I had now come to live and work. In order to understand my reaction, it has to be remembered that the 1950s was a totally different world from the one we are living in today. Women's magazines emphasised the romantic ideal of marriage and family, in which the man was the breadwinner, and the wife was the homemaker and mother who spent her days caring for house and family and had her husband's supper on the table when he came home from work and his slippers in front of the fire after the meal.

Illegitimacy was regarded as a cardinal sin that disgraced the respectable family in all social classes. Girls who 'got into trouble' were sent off to a family member in the country to hide their pregnancy from the neighbours; or they were forced to live in homes for 'fallen girls' after which their babies were taken from them for adoption. One such home near my church I occasionally visited if there was a girl there from our youth club. They were sad places that always upset me. But this was 1950s Britain into which the 'Windrush Generation' brought a whole new dimension.

Colonial Slavery

My rapid learning curve introduced me to the legacy of slavery which was an entirely new field for me as throughout my education, from infancy to university, I had never been taught anything about the 300 years of British colonial slavery. If slavery were mentioned during history lessons it was usually related to the cotton and tobacco fields of America, as already noted in Chapter One, but there was never any reference to the sugar plantations of Jamaica or Barbados. In fact, there were very few studies of Caribbean life before the 1950s. One of the earliest that I read was Edith Clarke's study of the families in three selected communities of Jamaica, *My Mother Who Fathered Me*.[17] This introduced me to the type of society that I encountered when I visited the Caribbean in 1962.

My visit was sponsored by the British Council of Churches with the objective of establishing links between the churches in Jamaica and churches in Britain in areas where the migrants were settling. I also had the personal objective of carrying out a short piece of research on family and marriage that would enable me to have a greater understanding of the migrant communities of London among whom I was working. During the months I spent in Jamaica, I travelled from one end of the island to the other, from Kingston to Montego Bay, spending a lot of time among rural farming communities and talking with the people as well as community officials and church leaders. Throughout this time, I was given the services of a community worker who travelled with me and made introductions for me. I learned a great deal from her, and it was her influence that enabled me to talk to the people I wished to interview for my own research.

I was also privileged to speak in many churches as well as at community events in the rural towns, and villages where we travelled. In Kingston I visited some of the shantytowns in the toughest areas which visitors, especially overseas white people like me, never see. My social worker guide, however, insisted on having a police escort and there were certainly times when I was glad to stick closely to the burly sergeant who accompanied us. I was used to difficult and threatening situations in London, but I had encountered nothing quite like this among ganga smoking Rastafarians whose hostility towards me was quite open and scary.

Family Life

I was particularly keen to see family life in Jamaica because it gave the background to what I was seeing every day among the migrants in London who talked about their family back home. I noted that most

---

17   Edith Clarke, *My Mother who Fathered Me*, Allen and Unwin, London 1957.

of them claimed to have been brought up by their grandmother and this was a phenomenon that featured largely in Edith Clarke's study. I wanted to know why this was, particularly as I knew that African society was traditionally strongly patriarchal, and I wondered why Jamaican society appeared to be matriarchal; what were the different sociological factors that accounted for such a change.

Edith Clarke's study uncovered some interesting facts about concubinage and marriage. Married couples were only found to be in the majority in upper-class areas where land was owned and passed down the generations in much the same way as happened in Britain, although in Jamaica inheritance usually went down the female line from mother to eldest daughter.[18] Among middle income families concubinage was common. Edith Clark notes,

> Before embarking on marriage, both partners are expected to show that they have finally ended any previous attachments, and they must also be given time to demonstrate what is generally described as their 'intention to live together' or their faithfulness. There is no question, however, of postponing cohabitation until this devotion has been tested. In fact, it is firmly believed that the testing can be done only over a long period of living together.

Concubine Relationships

She continued,

> The period of free cohabitation, following as it may a number of experimental unions, is rationalised as a necessary trial of compatibility which is not only expedient but respectable, since it ensures the stability of the marriage which follows . . . Married people must not only believe, but know from experience, that they can trust one another, and this was impossible 'If you just "butt" up a man one day and marry him tomorrow'. The result of these attitudes is that the ceremony is often postponed until after the birth of all or many of the children. One marriage in our records followed a concubinage of 14 years during which six children were born.[19]

---

18 This was a throwback from the days of slavery when the woman was the stable unity in the family.

19 Clarke, *My Mother who Fathered Me*, 55.

This was confirmed by my own enquiries during my visit to Jamaica. I spoke to many couples who were living in long term faithful concubine relationships. None of them were in a hurry to get married, but they all said that their intention was to marry at the right time. That time would be when the children had reached adulthood and they themselves had achieved a level of economic stability required to take the ultimate step of marriage. Clearly for all the couples I spoke to, marriage constituted a higher status in society. It would be marked by a marriage ceremony in church followed by a feast which they were expected to provide and to which they invited all the members of their village and often neighbouring villages, as well, of course, their own kin group and children.

A concubine relationship is one of mutual agreement leaving each party with the ability to end it at any time. I remember discussing marriage with one couple who had been living in a concubine relationship from a number of years. I asked them why they didn't get married, and the woman said, "I live with him – he beat me – I leave him. I marry him – he beat me – I cannot leave him." The man in this relationship simply said to me pragmatically, "I marry her – I buy her shoes. I don't marry her – she buy her own shoes." At least they seemed happy together. It was working for them.

Marriage

Edith Clark reported:

> In Orange Grove, (the higher social status group) marriage is part of the class structure and is reinforced with strong social sanctions. By contrast there is no adult pattern of male conjugal or paternal responsibility in Sugar Town (the lowest social status group).

> Working class young people typically begin their mating career with extra residential relations of varying duration and publicity. According to folk tradition these unions should receive the consent of the girl's parents; but often they are clandestine. Particular unions may or may not lead to childbirth or to consensual or legal cohabitation; but when sanctioned by parental approval and public recognition, these extra residential relations provide an adequate institutional context for the young couples mating. They also ensure in advance

acknowledgement of paternity for any children begotten in these relations. During such mating, the young girl normally remains in her parental home until such time as she has achieved her 'womanhood' by bearing one or two children. Normally then she will be willing to set up a joint household with her current mate; and if their union later breaks down, she returns to her former home until she finds another.[20]

Grandmothers

In all these family units within working class areas in my own research I found that the grandmother was the one stable unit. In many interviews I was told similar practices of casual liaisons between young people which are smiled upon in the case of the boys; but the girls are always given strong warnings not to engage in sexual intercourse. When, at length, a teenage girl becomes pregnant her mother makes an enormous fuss scolding her and beating her and driving her out of the house. She usually goes to an auntie or other female relative in a nearby village and after a suitable period of days or weeks the relative goes to see the mother on behalf of the child and pleads with her to take her back. This takes place amid much scolding and loving gestures.

The chastened girl then re-takes her place in the family home and when her baby is born, she suckles it until weaning takes place, at which point her mother then takes responsibility for the baby and the girl goes back to work and resumes her place in society. She is then regarded in the community as having proved her natural fecundity and is an eligible young lady for a more permanent relationship. This may be achieved with the father of her child or with some other man with whom she enters into an agreement for cohabitation which, if it becomes a successful relationship will last for many years during which time they produce several children. Then in due course they will marry, probably around the age of 50 or even 60 so that they end their days on the highest possible social status available to them.

Marriage is the ultimate objective in all classes of society. In the highest rankings, marriage is essential, and cohabitation and

---

20 M.G. Smith, University of California, Los Angeles, in the Introduction to Clarke, *My Mother who Fathered Me* , xxxvii.

concubinage are strongly despised. The virginity of their girls is carefully guarded and all contact with a prospective young man is strongly chaperoned. The usual pattern is for a young man to call upon the young lady of his fancy, but he has no conversation with her, instead, he talks with her brothers, and the adults in both families negotiate the terms of the marriage. It is essential that she remains a virgin because if she were found not to be, she could be sent back to her family.

In all other classes of society concubinage is acceptable, with marriage later in life being the general expectation. Edith Clark summarises the role of marriage after concubinage thus:

> Marriage occurring after a period of cohabitation is, in other words, the affirmation of stability; the seal on a proven conjugal union.[21]

Marriage in the Windrush Generation

The original 'Windrush Generation' in Britain of the first 10 years, from 1948 to 1958 was mainly male. There were few women and children among them. They were mainly men looking for work for a limited period, with the intention of returning home after a few years. Unfortunately, no figures for immigration were kept by the Home Office in Britain before 1955 so there are no statistics available to support these statements. Certainly, my own observations and records that I kept during that period show that the number of men greatly outnumbered Caribbean women in Britain. I wrote about the social problems I was observing in the early 1950s. Many of the men who came to Britain in this first wave of immigration were in concubine relationships back home where they had a partner and children dependent upon them. They regularly sent money home for the support of these dependants.

Life was not easy for these men living in cramped accommodation and having to do all their domestic chores, including shopping, cooking and laundry. In my own notes I recorded,

In these circumstances it may well be understood how readily a man accepts an offer of help from a coloured girl across the street, who is perhaps equally lonely and lost in the great metropolis where

---

21 Clarke, *My Mother who Fathered Me*, 57.

the whole of life seems to be so very different. He eagerly encourages a friendship with her and when she insists upon marriage as the price of her services, he not only feels that it is a small price to pay for the comfort he so dearly desires, but there are no legal ties to prevent him from taking a wife. He then marries his new partner and babies begin to arrive. With the new responsibilities and fresh demands upon his wage packet, he is quite unable to send his usual support to his family back home in the Caribbean.[22]

By 1958 the whole pattern of immigration began to change and men coming from the Caribbean were actually in the minority. There are no statistics available to show exactly when this change began because immigration was unregulated until July 1962. At that time figures published jointly by the Department of Employment and Productivity and the Home Office, showed that in the six months, July to December 1962, the number of those arriving from the Caribbean with work vouchers was 4,217 and roughly double the number of dependants arrived: 8,218.

It was from the late 1950s and early 1960s that the permanent migrant population in Britain began to emerge. At the time of the 1961 national census I noted that, 'The Ministry of Health estimated that about 35% of the coloured population in Britain are children under 16, of which more than half were born in this country and would be enumerated in the census, not with the immigrant minority, but with the general English population.'[23] It is factors such as this that make it extremely difficult to estimate the numbers involved in the family problems we are noting in the early days of Caribbeans living in Britain.

Marriage and Morality

In *Black and White in Harmony* I noted that there was a great difference between the moral values of members of Pentecostal sects and other young Caribbeans who claimed to be members of other churches. I noted an example that highlighted a number of the problems that I encountered among the 'Windrush Generation' in regard to sex and marriage. I wrote:

---

22 Hill , *Black and White in Harmony,* 76-77.
23 Hill , *Immigration and Integration,* 27.

I have known several men who have been completely ostracised by fellow members of their home church for having broken a taboo (on sex outside marriage). I was very sorry to lose one man from the church, who lived with his brother and was a particularly likeable and friendly boy. I had placed them both in suitable employment and they, unlike many others, showed their gratitude in many ways and were very regular in church attendance and faithful to my mid-week gospel meeting. I missed the two brothers from church for a couple of Sundays, following which I received a visit from a young Jamaican woman who stated that she was going to have a baby and that one of my congregation was the father. She wanted me to see the man and arrange for him to marry her, which he was at present refusing to do. I was more than a little surprised to learn that it was the younger of these two brothers whom she accused of being the father of her unborn child.

I took the first opportunity of calling on the two lads who shared a room in a large rambling old house somewhere in the Paddington area. On the first attempt I only succeeded in seeing the elder of the two brothers, but it was plain from his overanxious and embarrassed conversation that this was the reason for their absence from church. When I eventually saw the younger brother, he agreed that he had allowed this young Jamaican woman to visit him in his room on several occasions, but he said that he had since found out that she had a number of similar associations with other men. He himself, even if he was the father of her child, was not in a position to marry as he already had a wife and child at home in Jamaica, whom he was supporting by sending regular allotments home. There was nothing I could do towards a permanent and happy settlement of this problem, except to see that the girl was cared for until her baby was old enough to be looked after by a foster mother and she was strong enough to resume work.

The two young men never got over the scandal which this affair caused among their friends in the Pentecostal sect where they were attached in Jamaica, some of whom were in my congregation. They had so ostracised the lads that in spite of all my efforts, we never again saw the two brothers in church.[24]

---

24 Hill, *Black and White in Harmony*, 80-81.

Social Issues

In the 1950s and early 1960s the major problems we encountered among Caribbean migrants were family issues related to the change in social conditions from those that existed in Jamaica and other parts of the West Indies and conditions in Britain. It was not until after my own Caribbean visit and the research I had carried out in Jamaica that I really began to understand the issues involved in terms of family and marriage. Of course, I had noted the high level of illegitimacy among Caribbean immigrants which was certainly in contrast to social mores among white people in Britain of the 1950s. But I had not understood the issues involved, or the links with colonial slavery, or the social patterns that were evolving in that era.

Concubinage, for example was unknown in the UK and cohabitation was also virtually unknown in pre-1960s Britain. It is probably difficult for young people today to imagine what life was like in those days, but there were strong social pressures against, not only cohabitation, but sexual intercourse before marriage. In fact, the rate of births outside marriage in the 1950s was less than 5%: it did not exceed 10% until 1980. Family and marriage were very stable in the UK in the 1950s and the divorce rate remained low even in the mid-1960s.

It was the Divorce Reform Act of 1971 that marked a major change in Britain. The comparative figures for divorce in that period were:[25]

> 1966 32,000
> 1971 110,000
> 1991 220,000

This gives some understanding of why social workers in the 1950s found it so difficult to understand the issues when dealing with migrants from the Caribbean. They did not know the background of the young women who became mothers and had no experience of child-rearing which would not normally be their role in the Caribbean. Without the support of the extended family that they enjoyed at home they experienced considerable hardship, especially if the man they had married or with whom they were having a relationship, deserted them when they became pregnant.

---

25   Quoted from Clifford Hill, *Shaking the Nations,* Kingsway Publications, Eastbourne, 1995, 111.

Absence of Grandmothers

In Britain, very few older women came over as part of the 'Windrush Generation', so the absence of grandmothers was a major factor in the early days of the development of the migrant communities. Life was extremely hard for many young Caribbeans in Britain who had no man and no close family to support them.

Having both to work and to care for an infant in many cases resulted in extreme hardship. They sought foster mothers or childminders so that they could go to work and provide for their daily needs, but in those early days these were hard to find. The best they could usually do was to find another Caribbean woman with several children of her own who was willing to be a childminder during the days to make it possible for young single mothers to go to work. In cases where there was demonstrable child neglect, social workers had to intervene, but they too, found it very difficult to find foster parents for migrant children. It was even more difficult to find adopters for black children. In 1960 the Barnardo's Homes were reported to have 30% of their children hailing from Caribbean mothers. At that time, I wrote, 'The coloured woman does not have the same opportunities as the white girl to have her baby adopted. I know of no single case where a coloured child has been adopted either by an English or West Indian family.'[26]

There were long lists of childless couples wanting to adopt a child, but it was very hard to find a family willing to adopt a black child in the 1950s or early 1960s. In my own records I said,

> I have sometimes been able to provide foster mothers from among the women in my church, but the requests have always far outnumbered the ladies who are able to undertake the task of caring for a tiny baby during day times while its mother is at work. It is not easy for a Jamaican girl to have her baby cared for in one of the Borough Day Nurseries where vacancies are few and much sought after. I have known Jamaican girls, who are unable to go to work because of their young babies, living on so little that it has been a wonder that they have survived starvation. There was an urgent need for more welfare work among these girls who were often too shy

---

26 Hill, *Black and White in Harmony*, 83-84.

and too proud or too lost in this vast and baffling metropolis to even avail themselves of such welfare services as were open to them.[27]

Irrational Prejudice

Many of these social problems at that time were exacerbated by irrational prejudice. In a book published in 1965 I recorded the words of a schoolteacher who claimed to be a practising Christian and a regular churchgoer. She told me that during her summer holidays she acted as a 'holiday auntie' at a children's home where she relieved the regular matron. She told me that there were a number of little coloured children in the home and one in particular with whom she became quite friendly. One morning the little five-year-old Jamaican boy came running into her bedroom and after a few moments climbed into bed with her. She said,

> At first, I was delighted to see him, for he was a friendly little lad, but when he climbed into my bed, I suddenly went tense and shuddered all over. Even at the time I was angry with myself, for I longed to put my arms around him and cuddle him, which was what he both wanted and needed. Yet I felt I should scream if his black skin touched me, and some irresistible force compelled me to get out of bed.[28]

These weird ideas and irrational prejudices about colour were quite prevalent in Britain in the 1950s and 60s. They were part of the heritage of British superiority and false biological teachings on race. In the same book I reported another woman saying,

> My small daughter came home from her Sunday School quite recently with a missionary leaflet with a picture of an African boy tending some goats against a background of mud huts and village paraphernalia. The story described his life and ended with *'Aren't you glad that you are not a little African boy?'*[29]

About that same time, I remember reading a story in a children's book by Enid Blyton about a little African boy she called 'Sambo' who

---

27   Hill, *Black and White in Harmony,* 84.

28   Hill, *How Coloured Prejudiced is Britain?,* 55.

29   Hill, *How Coloured Prejudiced is Britain?,* 56.

was black, but when he ran through the magic rain it all washed off and he became white, much to the delight of all his white friends. It was this sort of racial teaching given to our children in former generations that strengthened racial prejudice.

Treatment of Minorities

My own experience of living and working among members of the 'Windrush Generation' enabled me to form many lasting friendships, some of which have endured until today. It has been a privilege to see into their personal lives and to gain some understanding of their experience of life in Britain and being part of a minority group that suffered a wide range of disadvantages. In the 1970s there was a spate of problems due to what was known in the East End of London as the 'Sus Laws'. This was the police practice of arresting people 'on suspicion' of having committed, or intending to commit, a felony.

In order to deal with what was seen as a crimewave, the police were given additional powers of arrest on suspicion without having firm evidence of the commission of a crime. This led to many injustices and a large number of incidents of innocent people being stopped and searched due to the colour of their skin. I was called to local police stations on many occasions when such incidents occurred, and the victim used their right of making a telephone call to appeal to me for help. Such incidents even included leaders of local churches whom I knew very well who had been arrested and taken to the police station largely because of their strong protestations which were interpreted as resisting arrest.

There were also occasions of wrongful arrest due to mistaken identity. One young man was taken forcibly out of his bed in a very early morning raid when the front door was broken down when the police were looking for a drug dealer. The man they were seeking was not at home and it was his brother whom they falsely arrested with such violence that they knocked out his front teeth. He was a young man whom I knew very well as a leader in a local church. Of course, I made a great deal of fuss about this and actually extracted an apology from the police for him, but this was small compensation for the shock and pain he received. It was incidents like this that caused me to look more carefully at the whole issues of prejudice and treatment of minority groups.

Legacy of Slavery

In our church in Tottenham where we began ministry in 1957 there were many people from the West Indies; a few from East Africa, but rather more West Africans from Nigeria and Ghana. Monica and I have a special concern for Nigeria which we have visited many times and where we have many close friends including an adopted son and daughter-in-law. We adopted him when he was a 13-year-old orphan who wrote to us appealing for help to complete his education. We brought him over to England to live with our three children and eventually put him through college after which he returned to Nigeria and he and his wife are now leaders in a church near Lagos.

The Nigerians in our Tottenham church formed a fellowship and spent a lot of time working on the constitution and devising their own rules and regulations, monitoring their activities. We had an even larger number of people from different West Indian islands and territories in a Caribbean fellowship. They were much less organised than the Africans and more easy-going which led us to study the different groups and to try to understand the differences. Comparisons were not very meaningful because the overwhelming majority of Africans in our fellowship were students, whereas almost all the Caribbeans were economic migrants fleeing unemployment and poverty.

Africans

The Africans mainly came from quite wealthy families who were able to support them and pay their university fees. But there were also strong social and cultural differences. The Africans clearly came from patriarchal societies whereas the Caribbeans were from a matriarchal background. We found it very difficult to form any kind of social interaction between the Africans and the Caribbeans. They were different in almost every way, and they simply did not mix. Indeed, the Africans were proud that they had never been slaves and they often denigrated the Caribbeans as descendants of slaves. They conveniently overlooked the fact that their ancestors sold their fellow Africans to the slave traders.

There were not only economic and social differences and cultural issues that interested us greatly. The Africans came from tribal communities with long histories of family traditions whereas the Caribbeans were quite unable to trace their family histories back beyond the days of slavery to their African tribal origins. All that was stripped from them by the devastating experience of 300 years of colonial slavery. The first thing we noticed was that none of the Caribbeans had African names; they all had English names – the product of slavery, which stole every part of their previous history including their culture, their tribal ancestry, their language, their personal identity, their names, and their freedom. They were given the name of the estate owner, so most of their names are English or Scottish, which is the permanent branding that they all bear to this day.

Caribbean Origins

Almost none of the Caribbeans wanted to talk about slavery. There was great shyness and reluctance whenever it was mentioned, and it was a long time before we had established sufficient trust with individuals to be able to talk freely on the subject. But the longer we lived and worked alongside people of Caribbean origins in London the more we recognised the practices of plantation slavery in the patterns of behaviour in the migrant communities of Britain. The outstanding examples were to be seen in the issues of family and marriage.

When we first began to speak about the legacy of slavery it was peremptorily dismissed by many white English people as being ridiculous. It was pointed out that slavery ended in 1838 which was several lifetimes ago and it surely could not still be affecting people in this generation. But our experience of many differences between Africans and Caribbeans – people with a common tribal heritage – could only be accounted for by colonial slavery. It was the only major sociocultural variable.

M.G. Smith in the introduction to *My Mother Who Fathered Me* wrote:

> It is to Orange Grove and Mocca (the more affluent groups with higher social status) that we have to turn to find examples of fathers lavishing care and affection on their children and carrying out conjugal and paternal duties.[30]

---

30   M.G. Smith in Clarke, *My Mother who Fathered Me*, xxxvi.

This is a remark with massive social significance, not only for understanding sociocultural issues in Jamaica, but for a study of Caribbean immigrant communities in Britain as we will see. The majority of the people in these more affluent groups were of mixed-race origin, with more European features and lighter skin colour. They were the product of plantation slavery and white oppression.

Brutality

In almost every aspect of family and marriage in Jamaica and other Caribbean islands the social patterns of slavery can be seen. It was the evil 'Slave Trade Triangle' that set the pattern of sex relationships between white Europeans and black Africans. James Walvin comments:

> The brutality of sexual relations on the slave ships was only another aspect of the violence endemic throughout the slave trade. The crudity of sexuality on the slave ships established the pattern which was to recur throughout the slave colonies, of an unbridled and aggressive white sexuality towards slave women which was ubiquitous and difficult to resist.[31]

> On most plantations in Jamaica, and especially in Barbados, slave women greatly outnumbered the men. The women proved a temptation which owners and overseers found very attractive; they were the sexual playthings of the white men who simply took their pick of the women regardless of the woman's existing relationships.

> Normal family life in the slave quarters was impossible. It varied from plantation to plantation, but long-term relationships between a man and a woman could never be guaranteed against separation. At the whim of the owner or overseer either party could be sold on the slave market and they would never meet again. This established the impermanence of family relationships among the slaves, although there were changes after the abolition of the slave trade when fresh supplies of slaves from Africa no longer came.

---

31 James Walvin, *Black Ivory: Slavery in the British Empire*, Blackwell, Oxford 2001, 189.

The owners began to increase the numbers of their slaves through natural reproduction, encouraging the strongest males to sire as many children as possible. As the number of infants grew, the younger women continued to toil in the field gangs, but the older women were employed as childminders which firmly established the role of grandmothers in the Caribbean family, which is still a major characteristic of Caribbean family life today.

In working class society in Jamaica, when I was there in the early 1960s, there were many stories about the predatory males taking any women they fancied. Stable families with a man and woman and their children domiciled together were relatively rare in the younger age groups. Cohabitation was more characteristic in working class groups and concubinage was the usual form of family life in the more stable middle classes. But, as we have already seen, marriage in any but the higher social classes was rare until later in life.

Commonwealth Immigrants Act 1962

All these cultural differences could be seen replicated in the immigrant communities in the early days of the migration to Britain, but they were ignored (or were unrecognised) both by social workers and by British lawmakers when framing the Commonwealth Immigrants Act 1962 which set up three types of work vouchers for immigrants, all of which were quite hard to obtain. The **C** vouchers for unskilled workers were strictly limited in number and were abandoned in 1964. The Act also gave an absolute right of entry to the wife and any child under 16 of a Commonwealth citizen who accompanied him, or her, to the UK. Dependants admitted were:

- A child under 16 coming to join a close relative or parent.

- The fiancé or 'common law wife' of a man settled here.

- The fiancé or 'common law husband' of a woman settled here.

- The widowed mother or elderly parents of a person settled here.[32]

---

32 Hill, *Immigration and Integration*, 12.

The common-law spouse was not recognised under British law, so they were regarded as fiancés. But this carried the intention to marry which had to be carried out within six months in order to fulfil the terms of admission. This put an immediate pressure upon those who came under this arrangement and many of those who came to me requesting a wedding showed signs of stress. Marriage carried social responsibilities for which some of the young men were not prepared, but it was forced upon them by the regulations. This led to many unhappy domestic situations and a breakdown of relationships with disastrous consequences for a whole generation of children born into unstable family situations, living in overcrowded and unsuitable accommodation.

The Second Generation

This is the social tragedy of the second generation that followed the 'Windrush Generation'. Of course, there were many successful marriages of couples who adjusted to the situation in Britain and established a stable family life. But, from my own observation and records, a significant proportion of these marriages and cohabitation arrangements broke down with men unable to settle, leaving women to care for the children, very often under very difficult circumstances. It is therefore small wonder that there was a high rate of juvenile offences in that generation and an overrepresentation of Caribbeans in British prisons still persists.

Monumental Injustice

Many of the first generation born in Britain were raised in conditions of poverty and hardship lacking the love and care of stable family life; never knowing the care of a father and having no male model to guide them. In the 1990s I visited the Feltham youth offenders' institution on numerous occasions where I was told that almost a hundred percent of the boys there had no visits from fathers and no experience of a stable adult male who loved and cared for them. This kind of instability continues down the generations as those brought up in unstable homes are unable to become stable parents themselves, so the problems escalate from generation to generation which is the situation that we find in many communities today of Caribbean people in Britain. **This is part of the legacy of**

slavery that can be seen in Britain today and it is a monumental injustice that is not recognised or acknowledged.

The call for reparations has been steadfastly ignored by politicians of all parties in Britain. But how much longer can we go on ignoring the evidence that is in front of our eyes of the effects of 300 years of slavery upon the people of the Caribbean islands and territories?

The legacy of slavery, however, is not confined to the patterns of family life and its effects upon the health and education of successive generations of young people. There is a much wider legacy that white superiority has given to the world – it is to be seen in the 'Colour Code' that dominates the lives of vast numbers of people today. It is this 'Colour Code' whose origins are examined in the following pages.

Chapter 7
THE BRITISH EMPIRE AND COLONIALISM

The purpose of this short chapter is to establish the background that colonialism contributed to the formation and systematisation of racial attitudes in the white dominated culture of Britain prior to the Second World War and the coming of the Windrush Generation in the early post-war period.

Background

The background and development of colour prejudice as part of the British heritage is rooted in the period of colonial expansion which was the forerunner of the imperialism which characterised the 19th century. By the middle of that century, Britain's Overseas Territories were very considerable and included India and large parts of Africa, while the latter part of the century was notable for the parcelling out of the remainder of black Africa amongst the European powers; and for the growth of the imperialist myth that Britain and her navy ruled the world. The sun never set on the British Empire.

The rationalisation of the expansionist policy driving Britain's international Empire was to be found in the belief that the European was divinely appointed to rule non-Europeans, for their own enlightenment and well-being. This was supported on the biological side by the application of cultural Darwinism to racial myths (e.g. Aryan) which affirmed the superiority of the white races and attributed biological inferiority to the non-white races. This political and biological concept of white supremacy was reinforced by a distorted version of the Christian religion which gave divine sanction to imperialism as a necessary foundation for missionary enterprise and evangelism, looking for the day when Jesus would reign over all the world – aided, of course, by the British. Indeed, the British Empire was founded upon this belief.

Trade Expansion in the Empire

The East India Company that was incorporated by Royal Charter in 1600 was formed with the express purpose of taking over the Indian spice trade from the Spanish. This was made possible by the defeat of the Spanish Armada in 1588 and the power of the British Navy around the east coast of Africa. The company began transporting slaves from East Africa to India and Indonesia which was then in the hands of the Dutch. The company's original objectives were purely for the development of commercial trade, but political activity became essential for the success of its ventures. Through the Regulatory Acts of 1773 and 1784 initiated by William Pitt the Younger, the British Government took political responsibility for India and made it part of the British Empire.

In 1793, when the East India Company Charter came before Parliament for renewal, William Wilberforce made a strong attempt to make it possible for missionaries to be sent out to evangelise all areas of India under the control of the East India Company. But this was strongly resisted by the company directors whose representatives in Parliament defeated the proposal. The charter did not come before Parliament again for another 10 years, but by this time Wilberforce was ready for them and he broke new ground for Parliamentary procedures.

Wilberforce and his friends in the Clapham group[33] were actively involved from the 1790s and through the early years of the 19th century in the establishment of charitable societies to help in providing social care for those most in need, and for the advancement of the Christian religion. They founded many religious groups such as the London Missionary Society in 1795, the Church Missionary Society in 1799, the Religious Tract Society in the same year, the Society for Promoting the Religious Instruction of Youth in 1800 and the Society for the Suppression of Vice in 1802, the Sunday School Union in 1803 and the British and Foreign Bible Society in 1804.

---

33 Long after Wilberforce's death the group of parliamentarians and abolitionists became known as 'the Clapham Sect' although they were all Anglicans including John Venn the vicar of Clapham. The term was meant to be derogatory and referred to their strong commitment to the Christian faith.

These societies recruited a wide range of supporters in towns and rural communities throughout the country. It was Wilberforce who was the first to perceive the value of these community associations for lobbying Parliament. By 1813 when the East India Company Charter came up for renewal, his Parliamentary campaign was in top gear. In county by county across the country the voluntary associations were used to recruit signatories on petitions to Parliament in support of Christian missionaries being sent out under the cover of the East India Company to take the gospel to the people of India.

This was the first big missionary undertaking in Britain, and it caught the public imagination powerfully. The combined petitions amounted to some 1.5 million signatories in a population of some 9 million. This was impressive by all accounts. Wilberforce himself made one of his greatest speeches lasting nearly 3 hours with compelling oratory that produced a parliamentary majority. It was a triumph for a new form of 'people-power' in parliamentary procedures.

Missionary Societies

The 19th century was characterised by the growth of missionary societies, and the enormous expansion of overseas missionary activity by European Christian churches. Although the missionary zeal in Britain and other European states went alongside the commercial activities of Empire it was also characterised by an attitude of European superiority that was common to all political imperialists.

The white man was thought to be divinely appointed to go overseas and take the light into the dark continents with their superior intellect. They were called by God to release the savage from the bondage of evil superstitions, and the horrifying customs of primitive humanity. This spirit was well expressed in the missionary hymn that was sung with great enthusiasm in churches of all denominations in the 19th century including both of my first two London churches, in Harlesden and Tottenham in the 1950s and 1960s. The popular hymn was:

> From Greenland's icy mountains,
> From India's coral strand,
> Where Afric's Sunny Fountains
> Roll down their golden sand,

From many an ancient river,
From many a palmy plain
They call us to deliver
Their land from error's chain.

Can we whose souls are lighted
With wisdom from on high,
Can we to men benighted
The lamp of life deny?[34]

White Supremacy

This kind of belief in white supremacy became endemic to European culture and was reinforced by missionary zeal and taught to our children so that it became an unquestioned part of British culture. A friend of mine who was a quantity surveyor and a civil servant quite high up in the MOD was given an official warning following a report he had submitted as an assessment on the work of a colleague in which he said: 'His work is surprisingly good, for an African.' He really could not understand why that was offensive and he thought it was an act of injustice that he was reprimanded. He thought it was an honest assessment and he could not see that it was a racist comment. White superiority is so much part of European DNA, and especially of the British, that it becomes difficult to distinguish it from factual analysis. It became part of British patriotism that is generally accepted and acceptable in most sectors of society even today.

Patriotism

This patriotism is demonstrated annually at the last night of the Promenade Concerts which are not only staged at the Royal Albert Hall in West London for cultural enthusiasts, but also at open-air gatherings in Hyde Park, in Edinburgh, in Belfast, and in Cardiff where vast crowds gather to sing with great gusto popular patriotic songs such as 'Jerusalem' and 'Rule Britannia!' These songs remind us of the days of the great British Empire when Britain did indeed rule the world! Whether this will continue in the post-Corona pandemic

---

34 Hymn by Reginald Heber, 1783 – 1826, published in the Congregational Hymnary of the Congregational Union of England and Wales, London 1887.

era has yet to be seen. But the fact that the songs, generated at the height of the British Empire and expressing the spirit of that age, have lasted well into the 21st century is surely a demonstration of how that sentiment has become embedded in the national psyche of the English, if not necessarily the Welsh and the Scots, who each have their own brand of nationalism.

The use of words and phrases with a racial connotation comes so naturally to the English that we often do not realise the extent to which they have penetrated our vocabulary. There are many areas of Britain today where there are few if any black people living. But this was the general experience of all older people who grew up anywhere in Britain in pre-World War II days, when there were virtually no black or coloured people in the population. In fact, even today, it is only young people growing up in inner-city areas who come into direct contact with non-white people every day. When children of different racial backgrounds grow up together it minimises racist attitudes. Regular contact is the most powerful agent of culture-change. Those who never meet members of the black or Asian minority communities first-hand, base their social values upon the experiences of others reported in the media, which at best is subject to misunderstanding and at worst to the transmission of social media distortion.

Racism

In my childhood in a pre-World War II London primary school, children in the playground all regularly chanted racist jingles – without ever recognising that they were offensive. When they were 'dipping' to choose partners for a game it was a regular practice to chant 'Eeny, Meeny, Miny, Moe, catch a n . . . by his toe, if he hollers let him go, O. U. T. spells out!' The child to whom the word 'out' was chanted was the one who was picked. All this was just a regular part of life, when girls were given gollywogs for Christmas presents and everyone enjoyed performances of the 'Black-and-White Minstrels', where white men with blackened faces sang songs and danced, as part of acceptable entertainment which nobody ever thought might be offensive.

The 1968 film, *'Till Death Us Do Part'* and the popular television series that ran for many years, starring Alf Garnett, an evil tongued highly prejudiced East End London docker, characterised the racist attitudes of many people of that era. In the same year of the film, Enoch Powell, the long serving Conservative MP for Wolverhampton South-West, made a speech that infamously became known as 'the Rivers of blood' speech which was widely condemned as racist but applauded by others.

Race Relations Acts

The First Act

The Labour Government's 1968 Race Relations Bill was due to have its second reading three days after Enoch Powell's speech, and the Conservative Opposition had tabled an amendment significantly weakening the Act's provisions. The Bill was a successor to The Race Relations Act 1965 limiting the numbers of immigrants to be admitted to Britain from New Commonwealth countries. Few people at that time appeared to notice that the very fact that MPs were debating limiting the numbers of new immigrants showed that their presence in Britain was a social problem.

Enoch Powell's speech touched a nerve. *The Times* declared it to be 'an evil speech', stating 'this is the first time that a serious British politician has appealed to racial hatred in this direct way in our post-war history.'[35]

The Conservative Party reacted by censuring Enoch Powell, but his speech triggered a march among London dockers in support of Powell. This was a sociological phenomenon with left-wing workers demonstrating in support of a right-wing Conservative, but it showed the strength of racist opinion among working class people who were directly affected by incoming arrivals in the shortage of housing and employment in inner-city areas.

Colonial Slavery Hidden

It needs to be recognised that part of the problem of racism in the 1960s was due to widespread ignorance of the existence of colonial slavery in British history. As already said, in my own period of school education colonial slavery was never mentioned. It is worth repeating here because it is of importance to note the widespread

---

35 *The Times*, London, 30th April 1968.

public ignorance of colonial slavery that was revealed in research carried out in London at the 200th anniversary of the abolition of the slave trade in 2007 and published in *The Zong Report*.[36]

Racism as a subject was not usually discussed in schools and it became an endemic part of the British cultural heritage that was socially accepted without it ever being recognised. Our everyday speech used the term 'white' in reference to purity, wholesomeness, truth, and goodness. By contrast 'black' was used in reference to evil and wickedness – all things that were harmful and unacceptable in polite society.

I had not realised the extent to which my own everyday use of terms that might be offensive until I made a horrible gaffe during my visit to Jamaica in 1962 – the memory of which still makes me hang my head in shame. I called one day to see a senior civil servant whom I knew quite well. I breezed up to the enquiry desk in his government department and in a moment of misguided friendliness I enquired, "Is the big white chief in?" There was a long pause and then the startled receptionist replied, "Mr C . . . is the head of this department, but he's a ***coloured*** man!"

I was mortified, and I mumbled my apologies while trying to explain my error and making it even worse. It was one of life's most difficult moments that I have never forgotten. I really was utterly shocked that I could have been so stupid. But it showed me the extent to which concepts of colour have got into our everyday language and are so much a part of our culture. For me, it was a painful learning experience

---

36 *The Zong Report*, published by Issachar Ministries in 2007.

Chapter 8
SOCIOLOGICAL ROOTS OF COLOUR CONSCIOUSNESS

This is a highly significant chapter in which the origins of colour coding are explored and which are seen rooted in the iniquitous system of colonial slavery. It looks at its cultural origins and African roots, at the infamous Trade Triangle and the sexual depravity of the white plantocracy whose total dominance of the African slaves allowed them the complete freedom of sexual exploitation.

Cultural Origins

It would probably be true of every society to say that if we are to understand its characteristics and its culture, we need to examine its historical roots. There is probably no population where this is more necessary than those of the British Caribbean territories. In the United Kingdom where a substantial minority of its population originate from the West Indies, examining the roots of that migrant population is not an optional extra, it is a matter of the utmost necessity.

We have already noted some differences between the African migrants in Britain and those whose origins are in the Caribbean former colonial territories. The most sociologically significant variable is colonial plantation slavery, but a second major factor of differentiation is colour, although, of course, these two variables are interwoven. Most Africans in Britain are black, whereas among the Caribbean communities there is a wide variety both of colour and of facial features. These differences are all the product of slavery.

Forced Labour

In compiling the following analysis, it is our desire to draw attention to the roots of the colour code system as being part of the legacy of 300 years of colonial slavery during which Africans of different tribal origins were welded into a forced labour society under conditions of extreme cruelty and hardship. This was inflicted upon them by a small but all-powerful white minority plantocracy from the British Isles.

If we are to understand the psychological springs of colour consciousness within the individual, we must first examine colour as a *sociological* concept and investigate its phenomenological origins. It is impossible to understand any aspect of Caribbean society, either amongst those people who have emigrated to Britain, or amongst the indigenous population of the West Indies, without taking note of the roots of that society.

Due to the particular history of the West Indies, it is essential to take note of its social history, as well as the geographical origins of the population. Only such an analysis will enable us to come to any effective understanding of the present-day social structures in the Caribbean islands and the concomitant Caribbean migrant communities who have settled in Britain. It will also provide a background study of some of the socio-psychological pressures that are formative in the lives of the expats living in Britain.

The whole of West Indian society, in almost every aspect, has been indelibly and irrefutably shaped out of the mould of the iniquitous system of slavery. It is this legacy of colonial slavery that forms the essential sociological background, both of the population of the West Indian islands and territories, as well as of the immigrant population with its Caribbean origins in Britain today. It is for this reason that this study of the origins of the colour/class system is being undertaken. First, a few historical notes.

African Origins

The fact that men and women who were sold into slavery on the plantations of the West Indies came from Africa does not mean that they had a common heritage. The slave population in the Caribbean mainly came from the Gold Coast area, but soon the coastal villages became deserted as the terrified population fled to escape the barbarous tyranny of the slavers.

The Arabs, who were mainly responsible for raiding villages, then force-marching this human traffic to the West Coast, had to push farther and farther East into Africa in search of more and more victims to supply the ceaseless demands of the New World for slave labour for the sugar plantations of the Caribbean and the cotton fields of America.

The first Africans to be taken across the Atlantic were in the voyage by Sir John Hawkins in 1562. The first black Africans to be sold in Jamestown Virginia, by an English slave ship was in 1619. The ship was originally Portuguese but was captured by British pirates, who took their human cargo to Virginia. This was followed by the first African slaves to be settled in the Caribbean which was on the island of Barbados in 1625. The British slave trade then extended to Jamaica in 1655.

The Infamous Trade Triangle

It was from the mid-17th century that the British slave trade began to establish the Trade Triangle between Britain, the West Coast of Africa, the Caribbean islands and territories, and the journey home to Britain. Each leg of the triangle was profitable, carrying manufactured goods from the burgeoning British Industrial Revolution for trading in Africa. Then African slaves were carried across to the West Indies, or to British settlements in America; and then bringing goods such as sugar and cotton back to Britain, to feed the growing market at home.

We need not dwell on the terrifying casualties and cruelties involved in the capture of the slaves or of the indescribable horrors of their transportation across the Atlantic, or even on the ghastly inhumanities they suffered in being moulded into the patterns of plantation life under the whips of the drivers. The point that is here being made in this study is the importance of the diversity of origin of the Africans, who were soon to form the bulk of the population in the Caribbean islands and the territories of the West Indies.

Diverse Origins

The diversity of tribal origins among the people imported from Africa is well expressed by Henriques:

The fact that the African slaves who were sold in Jamaica came from a number of different tribes is of the greatest significance in the whole history and development of the island. It meant that differences of language and customs prevented them carrying on their original patterns of behaviour. This, coupled with the pressure which the slave owners brought to bear, to make their slaves fit into the mould of the estate, was sufficient to destroy most of their tribal culture . . . The mixture of tribes in the slave markets of Jamaica also led, in time, to mixed African-Caribbean types coming into being.

Today, the Jamaican African cannot be identified with any particular African tribal people; he is the end result of generations of the mixing of more than half a dozen tribes.[37]

The system of slavery upon which plantation life was built meant that the black man was entirely at the disposal of the white. This was rationalised by Europeans by many processes of reasoning which generally included the basic assumption that the black man was in some way not fully human. Even the grossest cruelties and the most savage system of punishments were rationalised and justified by an appeal to reason by those who stood to profit from the system as an early 19th-century study demonstrates:

A slave, being a dependent agent, must necessarily move by the will of another, which is incessantly exerted to control his own will; hence the necessity of terror to coerce his obedience. It is, therefore, by the gross operations of fear, or the dread of punishment, that Negroes are wrought upon to action; for love doth little, and shame less to produce that effect. A system of remuneration alone is inadequate, for the reward must be ever incommensurate to the service, where labour is misery, and rest, happiness.[38]

White People Held Total Power

In everything, white was might and white was right. The black man was at the bottom of the social ladder; a creature who was only barely human and therefore not to be accorded the full dignity of humanity. In any sale of property, in the West Indies, or when an entire estate came onto the market for disposal, the Negro slaves were classified under the heading of 'stock' alongside such items as 'mules and steers'. Being thus totally the property of the white man and entirely at his disposal, the whole of his existence was subject to the white man's control. He was not even allowed to express a faith in God, or to engage in an act of worship without the permission of his master.

This was clearly expressed in the Consolidated Slave Act of 1816: slaves were not permitted to attend a place of worship, or to engage in religious duties in their own habitation, without a special licence

---

37   Fernando Henriques, *Jamaica, Land of Wood and Water*, Macgibbon and Kee, London, 1957, 23.

38   H. Collins, *Practical Rules for the Management and Medical Treatment of Negro Slaves in the Sugar Colonies,* London, 1811.

from the magistrates. And for the crime of worshipping God without their master's permission they were always liable to punishment, as a Baptist missionary in Spanish Town lamented.

> O for the day when slavery shall not be
> Where England rules, but all her sons be free;
> When Western India, and Mauritia's isle,
> Loos'd from their bands, shall learn at length to smile,
> When COLOUR shall no longer man degrade,
> And Christ by all shall be alike obey'd.[39]

Sexual Depravity

The control which the white man exercised over the African slaves also extended to their family life and sex relationships. This is vividly illustrated by Phillippo:

Not only did the taskmaster torture the bodies of his vassals by the whip, but he also corrupted their morals by his licentiousness. There was no law either to guard the CHASTITY OF A FEMALE SLAVE, or to avenge any insult that might be offered to her violated honour. Nay more, the simple expression of nature on the part of a slave as he witnessed the ruin of his wife, his mother, or his daughter, by any of the white fraternity was legally prohibited, and an attempt to protect them might be punishable with death. Thus, as they had no protection in their domestic intercourse, so neither had they any security in their sympathies and sorrows. They were subject to punishment at all times, which was inflicted by various legalised instruments of torture, by the common stocks, the thumbscrew, the field stocks, the iron collar, the yoke, the block and tackle, and the cart whip.

For running away from severe usage, a slave was deemed rebellious and might be mutilated. Acts for which a white man would be only imprisoned were deemed capital crimes in a slave. If any event transpired which could be construed into an insurrection, these poor creatures were shot like wild beasts, or hunted down with bloodhounds. If they made the least resistance they were hewn to pieces; if taken, were doomed to banishment or hopeless imprisonment in chains. If actually concerned in 'treasonable' practices, they were condemned without trial, and expiated their

---

39   James M. Phillippo, *Jamaica – Its Past and Present State*, John Snow, London 1843, 161.

crimes by sufferings inflicted with the wantonness of cruelty never exceeded by the most degraded barbarians.[40]

Blaming the Women

There were many attempts to blame the loose behaviour of European men with African women upon the licentiousness of the latter, but it should always be remembered that it was the white man who was in full and complete control. From the moment they were taken on board the slave ships the women were under the total control of European men who raped them.

The rich Creoles[41] soon discovered the outstanding qualities of the African woman as a priestess of Venus. Beauty, rhythm, and all those mysterious magnetic forces which draw men to women had in this case to triumph over forbidding social barriers. It follows that, in the nature of things, only outstanding African women could hope to win in the struggle; and therefore, that the mulatto was the outcome of a process of natural selection on the maternal side. Labatt writes:

> It is a mistake to believe that we understand Negro beauty to consist in the deformity of their face, their thick lips, their flat noses. If this kind of taste was ever fashionable in Europe, it was never so in the islands; there, one asks for regular features. The Spaniards, above others, look closely into the matter, and they will not haggle over a few hundreds of dollars in order to secure a beautiful Negress.[42]

The blend was apt to make the 'Anonymous Visitor', a good connoisseur of feminine beauty, wax lyrical. Coloured women here (in Martinique), as in St Lucia and Trinidad, are a much finer race than their fellows in the old English islands. The French and Spanish blood seems to unite more kindly and perfectly with the Negro, than does our British stuff. We eat too much beef and absorb too much porter for a thorough amalgamation with the tropical lymph in the veins of a black African. Hence our 'mulatto' females have more of the look of a very dirty

---

40 Phillippo, *Jamaica – its Past and Present State*, 157.

41 'Creole' is a native-born person of any colour.

42 Jean-Baptiste Labatt, *Nouveau Voyage aux Isles de L'Amerique*, a book written in the ealy 1720s, republished by Kessinger and now available on Amazon.

white woman than that rich Oriental olive which distinguishes the haughty offspring of the half blood of French or Spaniards.'

The writer continued, 'I think for gait, gesture, shape and air, of the finest women in the world may be seen on a Sunday in Port of Spain. The rich and gay costumes of these nations sets off the dark countenances of their mulattos infinitely better than the plain dress of the English.'[43]

Hypocrisy

There was, in any case, a lesser distance between the white and the black than between either of them and the Indian. The beauty and supposed lasciviousness of the African women was too much for the white – whether Spanish, French or English. White men of all nationalities finding themselves in complete power over the African women simply took them as objects of sexual pleasure whenever the fancy took them. All kinds of excuses were made for their behaviour, but to blame the women for the uncontrollable sexual appetites of the men is surely hypocrisy.

A typical excuse was noted by Labatt: 'The attire of this baser sort of people of blackamores and mulattos is so light and their carriage so enticing, that many Spaniards even of the better sort (who are too prone to Venery) disdain their wives for them.' So wrote Gage of Mexico quoted by Labatt; while Labatt himself wrote of the mulattos of the French West Indies,

> Their numbers would even be bigger in our islands, without the punishments inflicted on those who make them; for Negresses are of their nature lascivious, and white men are hardly less so, and as they find it very easy to satisfy their passions with these creatures, one would see nothing but mulattos, where from many disorders might flow, had not the King met the danger by condemning those who are proved to be their fathers to a fine of 1000 lbs of sugar.[44]

Origins of Colour Coding

In the West Indies, the abundance of domestic slaves provided planters and their sons and employees with rich sexual pickings.

---

43 Anonymous author: *"Six Months in the West Indies in 1825'*, MDCCCXX11, 141.
44 Labatt, 'Nouveau Voyage'.

Observers recognise that it was all too easy for young men to 'acquire those vices of manhood' by proximity to the domestics. One lady writing about Barbados noted that 'the gentleman are greatly addicted to their women slaves and give the fruit of their licentiousness to their white children as slaves.'[45] What we are dealing with here is the origins of the colour coding system in the Caribbean.

Thus did family relations in the great house become confused and complex; slave children, offspring of white masters and their slaves, became servants to their half brothers and sisters. Throughout the Caribbean a new complex process was set in train, of the light-coloured offspring of such liaisons securing preferential treatment for themselves and their children, emerging into a full grown 'coloured' class by the last years of slavery. They distanced themselves by colour and style from the Blacks below them, but were never accepted as equals by the whites above them. 'Slave women knew that they could improve themselves, and enhance the prospects of their children, by relations with white men.'[46]

According to Walvin, 18th century Barbados had more women than men among its slaves which was unique at that time. It was the women who did most of the fieldwork as well as the domestic duties in the homes of the white planters. The field gang work was particularly hard, and he reports:

Of the 180,000 slaves imported into Barbados between 1700 and 1760, some 50,000 died in the first three years . . . Fieldwork on the sugar plantations was hard: the great body of the slaves, the field people on sugar plantations, were generally treated more like beasts of burden than like human creatures, since they cultivate the land, with no assistance from cattle, and suffer every hardship which can be supposed to attend oppressive toil.[47]

Sexual Exploitation

Whether the African women were employed in field gangs or as domestics, serving in their master's houses, they were liable for sexual exploitation:

---

45 Hilary Beckles, *Natural Rebels, A Social History of Enslaved Black Women in Barbados*, Published by Rutgers University Press, London 1989, 65.

46 Walvin, *Black Ivory*, 106.

47 Walvin, *Black Ivory*, 106.

Few planters could have been as sexually aggressive as Thomas Thistlewood. He took his slaves wherever he found them, in the fields, in the various plantation buildings, but most of all in his own house . . . In his home he ruled supreme, and any woman working there was likely to find herself pressed into sexual service for her Master's pleasure.[48]

The African women were always at risk of exploitation because the whole system of slavery was based upon the total control exercised by white people. It is here that we find the origins of the colour code divisions that we are examining in this chapter. Walvin writes,

It was natural enough that men without women would turn for companionship and sex to the women they lived and worked close to. But it is impossible to speak of normal or natural relationships in so abnormal a world as that of colonial slavery. There may have been cases where white men fell in love with a black woman, but for every such case we have scores of examples of sexual exploitation of the basest kind. Throughout the Caribbean islands white women were in short supply, especially on the plantations, and white men simply took their pick of the available slave women, often with no regard to age, condition, or the woman's existing relationships.[49]

Mores Ignored

All the evidence from many different sources show that whatever ties an African had within the slave plantation communities and whatever mores they had brought with them from family life in Africa, these were utterly ignored by white predators. It is essential to record these unsavoury facts of which there is abundant and detailed evidence that we do not wish to repeat in these pages. It is, nevertheless, essential to recognise the helplessness of the African women and their exploitation at the hands of white men which provides the backdrop to any discussion of the origins of the colour code system that has its roots in the Caribbean slave plantations.

---

48 Walvin, *Black Ivory*, 115.

49 Walvin, *Black Ivory*, 190.

Chapter 9
THE COLOUR PYRAMID

This chapter explores the origins of colour consciousness and the development of degrees of colour which have become systemic in the culture of the Caribbean population. Different degrees of colour are noted with their association with social status which became established through colonial slavery in all the Caribbean islands and territories.

The Beginnings of Colour Consciousness

Any examination of life in the British colonial West Indies presents a picture of unmitigated force and exploitation. A similar situation existed in the Spanish owned Caribbean territories and in investigating the origins of the differences in colour to be found throughout the West Indian islands and territories it is necessary to take note of their history. J.B. Morton, describing life in the Spanish territories, stated:

> It is quite usual for a Creole gentleman after dinner to send to the field for one of his favourite wenches, who is instantly hurried home and conveyed to his chamber (or if he has a wife, to some other apartment) piping hot and drowned with perspiration, in which condition he enjoys the savoury object; after which he takes a nap for an hour so, and she returns to labour till night; thus he takes one almost daily in rotation and roves with as much ease and dignity as a plenipotentiary through raptures of delight.

Moreton adds that, as a result of this way of life, 'In one family I have seen white, mestee, quadroon and mulatto children, all brothers and sisters playing together.'[50]

---

50 J.B. Morton, *The Fall of the Spanish-American Empire*, Collier, New York, 109.

Degrees of Colour

John Waller, an army doctor, who for health reasons was sent to the West Indies in 1820, is one of those who supports the rationalisation that had become common among the planters. They had become adept at attributing their own promiscuity to the supposed inherent licentiousness of the African women. 'From their debauched habits, the females are continually producing an offspring from white men . . . The young Mulatto and Mustee females frequently procure their freedom and that of their offspring, as the reward of their prostitution and fidelity . . .'[51]

Yet Waller himself provides evidence for the fact that the white man could and did purchase the sexual rights of coloured women:

One day I received a visit from a very respectable-looking woman, who waited upon me at my apartments in the hospital (in Barbados), and, after some preamble, laid open the motive of her visit. I should not, on my first arrival, have taken her for a woman of colour, but I was now sufficiently accustomed to the features of these people, to perceive that she was a mustee. She informed me that she had always lived very respectably as the *chere amie* of an officer of rank who had been long dead; he had purchased her and died of the fever, leaving her with a female child. Before his death, he had made her free, but her daughter was not included in the manumission.

The daughter was her slave, left to her by will. She had bestowed some expense and great pains on her education; and her daughter, who was virtuous, had refused some good offers because she did not feel a mutual passion. She, the mother, could not think of forcing her inclination. I was at a non-plus to divine what this story could lead to; but the good woman at length put me out of my suspense, by informing me that I had seen and several times spoken to her daughter, and she thought, as I was not yet provided with what is here considered an essential part of the establishment of every unmarried man, that I ought not to let slip the opportunity of possessing a girl who was greatly attached to me, and whose person was very superior to the generality of women of colour.

---

51 John A. Waller, *A Voyage to the West Indies*, Philips & Co., London 1820, 93.

The terms on which she proposed to part with her daughter were the following: that I should purchase her from her mother at £120 in local currency, which, she said was £20 less than she would fetch at a public venue, and that I could engage to free her before I quitted the colony. She observed also, as a greater inducement, that there would be no need to purchase the freedom of the children, as she herself was of the last degree of colour that could be enslaved, and that her children would necessarily be legally free, and entitled to all the privileges of white people . . . [52]

Colour and Status

This dialogue recorded by Waller is very revealing for the origins of the colour class system in the West Indies and its roots in colonial slavery. The different degrees of colour were influential in determining the status of each individual and the point at which they could gain their freedom. There is a reference here to *'the last degree of colour that could be enslaved'* but this is not elaborated, so there does not appear to be a clear definition

Marly also provides a similar testimony. He declares that

. . . He was incessantly importuned by the pickeniny mothers, to take a wife; and there was not an individual among them who had not someone of their young female friends to recommend for that purpose.

Such recommendations were perpetually sounded in his ears:

Why Massa Marly not take him one wife, like oder buckras? Dere is him little Daphne, would make him one good wife – dere is him young Diana – dere is him little Venus – dere is him Mary Magdalene, and dere is him Phoebe . . .

besides many others who were also specially recommended. In addition to which, much coquetry among the young damsels was displayed, and all their attractive qualities were shown for the same end.

While thus engaged, and before he had finished, he was interrupted by a rather strange sort of application, from an elderly

---

52 Waller, *A Voyage to the West Indies*, 94.

Negro woman, accompanied by a young Negro girl about 16 or 17 years of age, who said she was her daughter, requesting Marly to take this young girl for his wife – the girls who live with the white people being so-called.'

Without assigning any cause, he declined this obliging offer, but seeing that the mother and daughter were disappointed and chagrined, he made a trifling present to the girl, with which they went away, apparently pleased, leaving him at liberty to finish his letter . . . [53]

It is clear from all the evidence that we have from this period that Marly was a most exceptional young man. There could not have been many who refused to take what all the European men held to be their right.

European Promiscuity

The result of all this promiscuous behaviour of the European with Negro slave women was to produce a class of mixed colour or mulattos as they were generally known. The offspring of these illicit unions between European men and Negro women were given many privileges which were unobtainable to the blacks. They formed a distinct social class in Caribbean society in which the whiter they were, conveyed greater privileges. Nowhere do these distinctions appear to have been defined in law; neither did colonial law define at what stage of colour or degree of European blood allowed an individual child to be set free. The practices varied from estate to estate. It was a matter of discretion for the master or overseer of the Plantation.

The Masters could not allow their own acknowledged children who clearly had some of their blood in them, to toil in the fields under the whips of the drivers. The more noticeable was the degree of European blood the more privileges were extended to them. Hence there was a premium in reward of licentiousness, as Negro girls and women were keen to gain privileges for their children. The mulattos were quick to take advantage of their position. Morton had a very poor opinion of what he called 'mongrels'. He wrote:

---

53 Marly; *A Planter's Life in Jamaica*, Glasgow/London, 1828,

All mongrels, male and female, have a vast share of pride and
vanity, baseness and ingratitude in their composition . . . The
men, if born to estates or properties (as many are) are much
of the same nature as the illiterate white Creole men . . .
When those spurious cubs, having no trades, squander what
their infatuated parents bequeathed them, they turn out the
most thieving, pilfering vagrants; for never having practised
any industry, but beggared themselves by their profligacy and
dissipation, Creole fashion, they are quite ignorant ever after of
the ways and means to earn their livelihoods, industriously and
honestly.[54]

The Spanish Indies

This may have been true of Jamaica and other British Caribbean
territories, but it was not true of Trinidad, St Lucia and Grenada, and
other West Indian islands that came under the sovereignty of Spain
at this time. As Salvador da Madariaga points out:

The general picture in the Spanish Indies was quite different
because the offspring of the mixed unions was generally
absorbed into the crafts. But most mulattos lived on their
beauty, seeking to rise in the scales of colour. Moreover, should
the Negro woman be a slave, the offspring, by a freeman in
Spanish lands, was free. This, of course, created a kind of
premium on the mating with whites, already favoured by social
prestige, wealth and colour prejudices and advantages.[55]

In the British territories, however, the Mulattos were not given their
freedom; in fact, the Whites went to great lengths to ensure that the
people of colour did not attain to anything like a position of equality
with themselves. They were an inferior order of creation, in no way
on a level with the pure white stock of European descent. In many
ways the privileges which were extended to them were negative
ones, but care was taken to preserve the distinction between them
and the white plantocracy who were the true elite.

---

54 J.B. Morton, *West India Customs and Manners*, London 1793, 125 and 124.
55 Salvador da Madariaga, in Morton, *The Fall of the Spanish American
Empire*, 117.

Prejudice

Nor did even the people of colour possess immunities to an extent to justify their claim to freedom even in the most restricted import of the term. However wealthy or respectable, and some of them were equally so with many of the more privileged whites, their evidence was inadmissible in criminal cases, both against white persons and those of their own colour.

Legal Rights

The right of trial by a jury of their own peers, conceded by the British constitution even to foreigners, was denied to the people of colour. They were ineligible for the office of magistrates, or churchwardens, to serve on parochial vestries, to hold commissions in the black and coloured companies of the militia, or to sit on juries. To this catalogue of legally recognised disabilities may be added those created by the 35th section of the colonial statute, which enacted 'that no Jew, mulatto, Indian, or Negro, shall be capable to officiate, or be employed, to unite in, or for, any of the public offices therein mentioned.'[56]

Nevertheless, the privileges of being coloured as distinct from Negro were enormous. At least the people of colour were spared the indignities, savagery and inhumanities that were the daily lot of their darker skinned brothers and sisters.

Colour/Class System

Thus, it was during the period of colonial slavery that this yearning to be white began. It was a yearning that stemmed from the very bottom of the colour pyramid; although it may not have been so general, or marked, in the pure black. For him, of course, a longing for something so utterly unattainable was like wishing for the moon. It was the people of colour who suffered the greatest personal anxieties and greatest degree of insecurity concerning their position in society. They were always sensitive to the way they were treated by others. They expected respect from those below them in the colour code and acknowledgement from those who were equal or above them. Above all they looked for equal treatment from white people and they were easily hurt if their privileged position of social status was not recognised.

---

56 Phillippo, *Jamaica its Past and Present State*, 145.

The one thing that the European planters did during the period of colonial slavery, was to plant indelibly into Caribbean society, the system that has already been referred to as the 'Colour Pyramid'. They firmly established the 'Colour/Class System' which is still very largely in vogue today throughout the West Indies, even in these enlightened days.

Five Grades of Colour

In the post-abolition era, Phillippo, writing in 1843, soon after the abolition of slavery throughout the British Empire distinguished five grades of colour. He said:

> Five principal varieties are generally enumerated as descending from the original Negro stock – the sambos, mulattoes, quadroons, mestees, and mestiphinoes. But to these refined distinctions, the Spaniards added the 'tercirons' and the 'giveros'. These two distinctions they were said to have proscribed and banished as being of the worst inclinations and principles.
>
> The Dutch recognised gradations still more minute, and which they attempted to distinguish and designate by adding drops of pure water to a single drop of dusty liquor until it became nearly transparent.
>
> A sambo is the offspring of a black woman by a mulatto man. A mulatto is the child of a black woman by a white man. A quadroon is the offspring of a mulatto woman by a white man, and the misty is that of a quadroon woman by a white man. The offspring of a female misty by a white man being above the 3rd in lineal descent from the Negro ancestor, was white in the estimation of the law. All these enjoyed all the privileges and immunities of her Majesty's white subjects, but all the rest, whether mulattos, quadroons, or mestees, were considered by the law as mulattos, or persons of colour. A Creole, whatever his condition, or external peculiarities, is a native. Thus, it is customary to say, a Creole white, a Creole of colour, or a Creole black.[57]

---

57   Phillippo, *Jamaica: its Past and Present State*, 144.

The Spaniards were even more meticulous in distinguishing various grades of colour. These were 'Mestizos, Mulattoes, Sambos, simple mixtures of the three colours (European, Negro and Indian), two by two, mixed in their turn either with one of the two colours whence they came, or with the third colour, or with other mixtures.' The outcome was a rich palette of human blends, with an equally rich vocabulary to describe them.

There was hardly a combination of colours, a mixture of mixtures, without its own name; particularly those which marked the stages in the ladder from black to white; Mulatto, Terceron (Mulatto and White), Quarteron (Terceron and White), Quinteron (Quarteron and White).

The Rank Ladder

The cause of this wealth of names was the extreme touchiness of the parties concerned with high regard to their position on the social status ladder.

> Everyone gives so much importance to the rank or social class, and draws so much vanity out of it, that if inadvertently, one of them is treated as belonging to a degree lower than that to which he is entitled, he blushes and holds it as the worst insult.[58]

This observation of Ulloa and Jorge Juan shows to what an extent the whole society of the West Indies hung, so to speak, from its white apex. Some of the names given to the middle mixtures express it most felicitously.

The struggle between the sexes which we decorate with the name of 'love', acquired in the West Indies a new zest owing to colour differences. The dusky lady sought always to lose her heart to swains better placed than she was on the ladder of whiteness, and the swain as usual *fell* in love – for language gives us away.

Social Status

> The offspring was better off than the mother, but had to pay for this advantage by being worse off than the father. There were cases, however, in which Cupid won on his own account,

---

58 Jorge Juan and Ulloa, *Relacion Historica del Viage*, 1748, reprint edition 2018

paying no heed to black or white; cases in which six married half-a-dozen.

When Terceron married Mulatta, or Quarteron married Tercerona, the offspring neither gained nor lost, but remained in the same state of suspended animation. Its name expressed it admirably. The children of such marriages were known as 'Tente-en-el-aire' – 'Hold-yourself-in-the-air'. On the other hand, when a fairly advanced type, Quarteron or Quinteron married a Mulatto or a Negro, their children were known as - 'Salto-atras', 'Backward-leap'.[59]

Thus, successive generations throughout the period of colonial slavery, accepted the fact that to be black was to be totally devoid of privileges; a mere beast of burden who happened, as it were, almost by accident, to possess the same physical attributes in common with the rest of humanity, except the one that was of paramount importance – a white skin!

---

59 Salvador da Madariaga, in Morton, *The Fall of The Spanish-American Empire*, 124.

Chapter 10

HISTORICAL ROOTS OF COLOUR CONSCIOUSNESS

This chapter explores the sociological roots of colour consciousness that became part of the culture during the era of slavery and remains to this day. It notes the changes in legal position and the establishment of attitudes leading to the white pyramid of social status. We note how culture has followed the trends, and fashion has reinforced attitudes of prejudice in such matters as facial beauty and hair styles.

The curse of being black pursued the captured Africans taken to the Caribbeans and the Americas from birth to death. For many of them it was a death accelerated by suffering and brutality, or even brought about by their own hand. There were many who preferred suicide to continuing to live in the hell of the white man's world.

Legal status

If the black Africans' position was intolerable, the position of the people of colour was hardly much better. They had no franchise and, as has already been pointed out, they had no privileges in law. Their position was that of a subject-being, whose treatment was better than that of the Negro, purely as an act of grace and favour on the part of their white masters. Even those who attained their freedom, or were born free, could never hope to attain to the social position held by the whites.

By this time (1838 – when the slaves were legally set free), the coloured group was beginning to vie with the white planters for economic power, but although individuals might often be equal, or even the superior of the whites in terms of property, they were never accepted as social equals. The black section was economically the weakest in the community. The freedom of the Negro meant no change for him in the hierarchical system.[60]

---

60 Fernando Henriques, *Family and Colour in Jamaica*, McGibbon and Kee, London 1968, 38.

Emancipation

It was, of course, impossible to end a system so deeply entrenched into the general body of accepted ideas and customs of the whole population by a mere Act of Parliament. Emancipation could not possibly change the position of the black man in the social scale, overnight. Economically, he was hardly any better off; he had simply exchanged the role of white man's slave, for that of poor peasant-worker in a white man's world.

It is for this reason that the compensation paid by the British Government to the owners of slaves, to which reference has already been made, can be seen to be a great injustice. It seems almost unbelievable that Parliament, when considering the whole subject of emancipation should give so much thought to the compensation of those who were losing the labour of the African slaves, that produced the wealth with which they built their fine houses in Britain yet gave so little attention to the condition of the Africans they set free from generations of cruelty and oppression. It is an indication of how excessively economic considerations were gripping the British Parliament, that no attention was paid to the new mode of life facing the Africans as free men and women under the Crown.

No aid was given to the ex-slaves to establish themselves in agriculture or commerce. It is from this lack of economic planning and forethought in the immediate post-emancipation period, that so much of the poverty and unemployment has stemmed, which still bedevils most of the West Indian islands. This enabled power to be firmly established in the hands of the small white minority, plus a small number of wealthy coloureds, and this situation was to continue for most of the next one hundred years.

Franchise

In 1865, the year of the Jamaican rebellion, only 1,903 out of the entire population of 440,000 human beings had a vote. Of that number only a tiny fraction were coloured or black.[61]

After 1865, the position eventually changed. In 1938, the people of Jamaica were granted universal suffrage, while self-government was not achieved until 1948 more than one hundred years after the

---

61 Lord Olivier, *Myth of Governor Eyre,* London, 1933.

Act of Emancipation. This in its turn, was the prelude for independence within the Commonwealth, which was granted on 6th August 1962. The record of Trinidad, the second largest British West Indian island, has been much the same. She achieved her independence within the Commonwealth, later in the same month of that year.

Alongside these major political changes have gone social and economic changes hardly less revolutionary. The position of the coloured and the black man has vastly improved. Nevertheless, colour still plays a tremendously important part in West Indian society. Jamaica is fairly typical of the rest of the British Caribbean.

Social Hierarchy

The Jamaican does not wish to be reminded of slavery. Thus, it is a topic which is rarely discussed. People are aware of its existence in the past but see no reason to dwell upon it today. It is all too painful, so it is better to regard it as all over and done with. I introduced the subject in hundreds of conversations I had during my tour of Jamaica in 1962. Very few were willing to discuss colonial slavery: they dismissed it with the simple statement that it was all in the past and it was no concern of theirs today. One cannot say the same about colour. It is very much with everyone today. Colour dominates social relationships; it may help or hinder you in your job, or trade, or profession and your social position in society. In the light of all my conversations in Jamaica it was clear that colour was a major determinant of social status. At that time, I found that 'colour' determines your permanent position in the social hierarchy of Jamaica.

How has this come about? Who is responsible for the continuance of a state of affairs which should have died with slavery? The answer is very simple – **the Jamaicans themselves** – where attitudes to colour have become institutionalised and systemic. Of course, this is not to say that they are responsible for the existence of this colour code hierarchy. It was a culture that was imposed upon them. But they are the ones who continue to observe it.

The abolition of slavery did much to destroy the economic power of the planters. But there remained a small but powerful group of Europeans. At the time of independence in 1962, the Europeans in Jamaica numbered a mere 15,000. This was out of a population of approximately 1.5 million. But this tiny minority were hugely influential and held both economic and social power highly outstripping their numbers.

White Minority

The prestige and social position of the white minority was out of all proportion to their numbers. Many of them were still wealthy, although hardly in 18th century terms. Others were poorer than their black or coloured neighbours, but felt themselves vastly superior. There is something magic in the possession of a white skin in Jamaica, but it is a magic which can only work if everyone believes in it, white and non-white alike!

Generations of slavery, when to be white was to be free, and to be possessed of all the virtues, have left this legacy of paradox. All those who are not pure white, and that is the vast majority of the population in Jamaica, are constantly striving by every means in their power to emulate and imitate the European. Just as in the days of slavery, the coloured estate owner would try to outdo his white neighbour, which was often seen in such things as the severity of his treatment of his slaves; so today, the fair skinned individual will have as little as possible to do with his darker skinned neighbours, lest he be associated with them in the minds of the whites, or fair-skin neighbours.

European Ideal

The important point is that all the different groups, from black to the white, accept the idea that the European is the ideal, and the Negro is inferior. This, of course, is rarely expressed openly. A suggestion from a visitor to this effect would be angrily denied by a person of any colour, but there is a great deal of evidence which supports this contention.

In Jamaica, Negro features, hair, and colour, are termed 'bad'. The more these characteristics approximate towards the European, the better they become. The use of such words, in itself, shows the ultimate bias.[62]

---

62 Fernando Henriques, *Jamaica: Land of Wood and Water*, McGibbon and McKee, London 1957, 127.

Thus, it is that all sections of Jamaican society have been responsible for perpetuating the myth of white superiority. The colour pyramid simply could not work without this universal support! If the dark-skinned man did not believe it was better to be fair, the glamour and prestige attached to the fair skinned person, would soon be stripped away. But how can such attitudes be changed after centuries of colonial slavery and many generations since emancipation have institutionalised the values that are embedded in society today?

Jamaica Today

The social and economic situation in Jamaica today, as in the rest of the Caribbean, has been undergoing radical changes since independence in the early 1960s. But the slowest social change has been in the area of attitudes to colour which determine the whole social class system. A major social change is that the really dark-skinned man is now getting opportunities that were never before open to him. For a first-hand view of the situation in Jamaica today, see Chapter 13 of this book written by my colleague the Revd Alton Bell who was born and raised in Jamaica.

Men of the darkest skin in Jamaica are now able to serve in all the professions, including becoming elected Members of the Government. They are also to be found in the Civil Service and in the social services, as Government employees. One area in which they are rarely found, however, is in the banks, where white and fair skinned employees usually occupy the front-line positions where they meet the public. The reason for this is not hard to determine. In the matter of caring for their money, the rich and powerful, prefer to deal with a white person, or a person of very fair skin. It is simply a matter of social prestige! It is also a demonstration that the legacy of slavery still exists in Jamaica – although few would dare to admit this!

Whether the example being set by the Government, as it is in Jamaica, will eventually affect the world of commerce and the whole of society, remains to be seen. At present, it is not only the banks, but also in major business houses and prestigious stores where their employees deal with the public, that staff are invariably fair skinned. At the time of independence, it was reported that if two persons of equal ability, one fair skinned and one dark, applied for the same job in Kingston, it would be the person of fair skin who was more likely to get the job. This may not be so true today, but the evidence of the colour-coded pyramid was certainly very evident when I visited Jamaica in 1962. It could be seen in ordinary everyday relationships.

Social Class and Colour

Class and colour have been indissolubly linked in West Indian society for hundreds of years. They are powerful social and psychological forces that in many ways control the values of multitudes of people in many different communities throughout the world.

It is not possible to effect a fundamental change in the values of a society in the course of a single generation. For many generations, to be white, or to be of very fair skin, has been to belong to the upper class, and therefore to possess privileges above and beyond the rest of society. Social values and culture change only takes place over a long period of time. As Jamaica only achieved self-government within the old British Empire in 1948, it was only 14 years later that independence was achieved and this is a very short time in which to effect fundamental social changes, so it was unlikely that I would see radical changes in my visit in 1962 shortly before independence was celebrated.

There is no overt legal discrimination between the races in the British West Indies, but racial prejudice asserts itself in a radical form on the social level. In the middle-class society of Trinidad, for instance, a dark-skinned brother in a fair skinned family is sometimes subjected to insults, and fair skinned girls who marry dark skinned men are regarded as having married beneath them. In West Indian island society, the surest sign of a man's having arrived, socially and economically, is the fact that he keeps company with people of lighter skin complexion than himself.[63]

A.A Campbell, writing in the 1960s said:

It is easier for a light-coloured man to make his way in the world both economically and socially, for the two fields of

---

63 For a good discussion on this subject see Matthew G. Lewis, *The Negro in the Caribbean*, Negro Universities Press, 1969, 60-69. Originally published by John Murray, London, 1845.

activity are inextricably intermingled. Advertisements for light-coloured shop assistants, domestic staff, and others are quite common. Some businesses only employ white employees, a few, notably the banks, chiefly employ white senior staff. So far as opportunities for social advancement are concerned, it is usual to find that the dominant partner in a marriage has 'married lighter' so as to 'raise the colour' of the offspring.[64]

Coloured Middle-Classes

T.S. Simey, also writing in the 1960s said:

A successful member of the coloured middle-classes may sometimes marry a white wife, but this is not by any means a frequent occurrence in the British West Indies. This can only be the source of deep feelings of frustration on the part of many coloured people, who may look with jealousy on the favoured positions which those with lighter complexion occupy in the community. These feelings may, indeed, become so intense that a single incident where a man suffers some public slight by reason of his colour, such as the refusal to allow him to occupy a berth on a ship, or admit him to a club, can do so deep an injury to him, that the structure of his whole personality may suffer serious and permanent injury as a result.[65]

Wealth

While it is true that money is a great leveller, and to be rich opens up avenues in society that would normally be closed to a poor man, the fair-skinned and the white people will not easily give up their privileges. On their side, as unwitting allies, they have all the deeply entrenched prejudices found throughout the West Indies amongst the darker skinned who have been taught for hundreds of years to look with envy upon the possessor of a fair skin. For generations it has been the ambition of dark -skinned parents to marry their children 'well'. Making a good marriage

---

64 This same phenomenon has been noticed in the American Virgin Islands. See A.A. Campbell, *St Thomas Negroes – A Study of Personality and Culture*, reprint London 2018

65 T.S. Simey, *Welfare and Planning in the West Indies*, Clarendon Press, Oxford, 1947, 98.

means marrying someone of a fairer skin and the term generally used for this is 'lifting the colour'.

A black peasant proprietor of more than average standing said: 'In the old days the mother of a black or coloured daughter, felt a sort of pride in her daughter living with the slave master – "Gone to buckra (Master) house, gone live".' This was reported by Fernando Henriques. Writing in 1968 he said that that feeling still applied. The black girl who co-habits with a white man had 'gone lift de colour'. He said: 'Mothers would rather their daughters lived with a brown or white man than marry a black man.'[66]

In any society where colour is an important factor in determining the scale of social values, people of all colours, except those at the apex of the colour pyramid, are bound to experience psychological tensions in regard to the colour of their skin. The very knowledge of one's social inferiority, or supposed inferiority, cannot fail to produce a psychological effect upon the personality of the individual.

African Culture

Again, quoting Henriques from his social research in 1968 where he found colour consciousness at all levels in society. He wrote:

> The coloured person in the West Indies, represents a unique phenomenon in the hybrid world. He is generally almost entirely ignorant of African culture and despises what little he does know as being primitive and connected with the undesirable, that is, the black. According to his colour, he is the prey of much anxiety as to whether he will be able to achieve, or has achieved, acceptance by the white minority. Even if this ideal is unattainable, there is still the conscious anxiety to appear white in his ways and ideas. The intensity of this anxiety varies from individual to individual but is apparent in all.[67]

From other sources it was possible to affirm the findings of Henriques, but it was perhaps even more noticeable in women than in men. Many women in the 1960s would go to almost any lengths to appear fairer or more 'European' in appearance than nature's original gifts to them.

---

66 Henriques, *Family and Colour in Jamaica*, 50.

67 Henriques, *Family and Colour in Jamaica*, 44.

Hair Styles

Once again, we turn to Henriques:

A phenomenon which is found everywhere there are Negroes in the New World, is 'hair straightening'. Ordinary Negroid hair tends to be woolly and crinkly. If the hair is subjected to a process, frequently repeated, of steaming and combing, it becomes straighter and flatter. In other words, it becomes more like the hair of a white person. Whatever black or coloured people may say about it, the fact remains that all over the West Indies and the United States, and more recently in Britain, hairdressers do a roaring trade in 'hair straightening'. In Jamaica you see the confirmation of this on every hand. It appears to be largely confined to women, possibly because male hair of this kind tends to be shorter, and thus less amenable to treatment. In connection with 'hair straightening' strange anomalies occur.

American Negro newspapers will carry advertisements for this process or that, relating to treatment of the hair, and in the same issue print articles extolling the virtues of black people, and their superiority to the whites. It seems difficult to avoid the conclusion that the general anxiety on the part of black and coloured women to achieve hair similar to the European is an admission of the latter's superiority . . . Hair straightening is not by any means a habit confined to the lower classes in the beauty parlours of Kingston Jamaica, and other towns; it can be an expensive process. The extraordinary number of so-called beauty parlours, and the number of girls who wish to adopt 'beauty culture' as a profession, testifies to the desire for good hair.[68]

Black is Beautiful

In Britain we have the strange anomaly of October being celebrated as 'Black History Month' when 'black is beautiful' is celebrated, while at the same time black women continue with their beauty treatments and hair straightening. More recently we have had the 'Black Lives Matter' campaign that began in America

---

68   Henriques, *Jamaica Land of Wood and Water*, 128.

and rapidly spread worldwide. Some of its objectives have been to celebrate blackness and raise the profile of black people and their achievements in sport, entertainment, the media and other high-profile activities. At the same time within Caribbean migrant communities in Britain hairdressers do a roaring trade in helping women to achieve a fairer complexion and more European hairstyles!

A photographer told me that he was very popular for weddings and other celebrations in the Caribbean communities in London because he had learned how to under-develop the photos he took to give a greater appearance of fair skin or whiteness of those who engaged him. I discovered that women sometimes use a pack made up of peroxide, clay, and Fullers Earth, which is worked into a paste and coated on the face. It is left on for about a quarter of an hour. The effect is supposed to be that of producing a light smooth skin. Unfortunately, whatever the effect, it does not last and the whole process has to be repeated some six months later.

Face Creams

In 1960s Jamaica, it was by no means uncommon to see face creams advertised as possessing the ability to make the skin appear fairer. Less subtle advertisements offered plain straightforward bleaching creams. On important social occasions in their lives, such as weddings, every self-respecting West Indian girl performs a meticulous toilet preparation for the great occasion, which normally includes straightening and then waving the hair. It also includes the application of face creams, often completed with a white face powder spread on top of the cream. The effect of this 'beauty culture' often gives a pallid appearance to the skin.

It is a strange comment upon the perversity of human nature, that in England most white girls long to appear suntanned or 'brown' as it is generally termed. They save throughout the year to pay for a package holiday somewhere around the Mediterranean where they can lie for hours exposing to the sun as much of their body as possible in order to get brown. If they are unable to go abroad to get the sunshine and achieve that greatly prized tan to their body, they will even resort to the use of sun beds or sunray lamps, or to the application of suntan lotions in order to darken the colour of their skin.

Wanting to be Different

English girls whose hair is naturally straight, will spend hours of time and much of their money at the hairdressers in an attempt to put crinkles and curls into their hair, by so-called 'perms', giving them permanently waved hair. It would appear that human beings are rarely satisfied with their lot. White people want to be brown and brown people want to be white. But no one wants to be black. We are all still prone to one of the most ancient of all temptations, against which the tenth commandment was directed: *'You should not covet your neighbour's possessions'*.

Colour and social class are closely bound together in many Western nations today – they are major social forces; but few people ever stop to think of their origins and to analyse the prejudices and ambitions that are the outcome of the colour class system. Few people stop to think of how their lives today are being influenced, and in many cases controlled, by a legacy of slavery that ended nearly 200 years ago but whose effects are still powerful social forces today.

Chapter 11
THE PRACTICE OF PASSING

This chapter notes the practical effects of the colour pyramid in the lives of people of very fair skin who are able to pass as white in a white dominated society in the USA. It notes how colour consciousness has moulded attitudes and behaviour of individuals and communities with examples of the effect upon people in mixed race populations.

'Passing' is one of the most prevalent practices that has arisen out of the American pattern of race relations. It grows from the fact that one known drop of coloured blood is sufficient to make an otherwise completely white person, black. There are many black people who only have a very small amount of coloured blood in their background so they cannot be distinguished from full-blooded whites.

> It is understandable that in the anonymity of the city, many blacks pass for white daily, both intentionally and unintentionally. But should white people become aware of their remote coloured ancestors, they would, in all probability, treat them as blacks.[69]

Embarrassing Consequences

A good example of the dangers and the possible embarrassing consequences of 'passing' was given by a young lady from Chicago whose skin colour was almost white in the following incident. It took place in the USA in the days before segregation was banished by law and black and white travellers on public transport travelled in different parts of the coaches. It is very informative for a description of life in the former slave states of the southern USA. The young lady recorded her story, saying:

---

69   St Clair Drake and Horace R Clayton, *Black Metropolis*, University of Chicago Press,Chicago 945, 159.

Speaking of passing – a strange thing happened to me this summer. When I went down to visit my father in Kentucky, I had to change trains at the station on the other side of the Mason-Dixon line. The porter took my bags and escorted me to the coach. I wasn't paying any attention to him. I just took it for granted that he was taking me to the correct coach.

When I stepped into the coach, I immediately knew that he had made a mistake. All of these people seated there were white, and so was I in appearance! I said, quietly, 'Listen, Porter . . .' And that's all that I managed to say. He interrupted, 'That's all right Miss, the conductor will call your stop.' He passed my bags overhead and tipped his hat and walked away. So, I sat down but I was so ill at ease. I noticed several of the white people glancing at me and then after the second look they looked off. I had my hair freshly done, and when it is fresh it looks dark brown and wavy, and I did look decent, because I was wearing my best. I took out a magazine and began reading.

After a bit, the conductor came up and after removing his hat and apologetically clearing his throat, he said, 'I know this is highly irregular, Miss, but – er – pardon me – may I ask you what nationality you are? Er – are you Jewish?' I could have kissed the conductor for giving me that lead, because as soon as he started talking, I knew what he was going to say. I knew that if I said I was a black and tried to explain that I wasn't trying to pass, he wouldn't believe it.

Also, to have to go back into the black coach with the conductor leading the way, would have been terribly embarrassing for me. The blacks would think I was trying to pass and got caught. So, I decided to play up to the situation. 'After all,' I said. 'This is highly ridiculous. Yes, I am a Jewess, and I consider this a grand insult.' I wore my hottest expression, but I was scared to death.

By this time several of the white people had turned around and were listening to us. The conductor flushed and was very much embarrassed. I just know how he much he must have felt. He apologised again, and then walked away. I was scared. I didn't enjoy the ride at all, and but for the company of a little eight-year-old white child, I talked to no one. It was lucky for me that I hadn't told my father that I was coming. Suppose he had been at the station to meet me – then I would have been in a mess. I told daddy about it and he just laughed. He thought it was a joke! And that's why I couldn't be bothered with trying to pass. I'd rather be coloured, and not be bothered. That's why I hate the South.[70]

Living in Two Worlds

As the above incident suggests, 'passing' in the south, in the days before segregation ended, following the assassination of Martin Luther King, could often lead to serious trouble because it violated both custom and law. There are numerous stories about the dashing young men from the northern states of the USA who came to a southern town, cutting quite a figure, perhaps, before becoming engaged to a socially prominent local girl, and then suddenly and mysteriously they disappeared, never to be seen again. It is discovered by accident in some instances, and so the tales go, that the man, though he appeared to be white, had black blood in him.

In the north, however, where the population was not so sensitised, and in the crowded and impersonal atmosphere of the big cities, little thought was given to the possibility that someone might be 'passing' and no punitive attention or action was taken by the society, even when a person was 'passing' and discovered.

To be very fair, or near white, in a white dominated and highly prejudiced society can be extremely disruptive to the normal flow of life and has its penalties as well as its privileges. It can lead to a person living in two worlds, with all the consequent schizophrenic pressures upon the personality. If a person is habitually passing for white in such a society, he or she must either take care to completely dissociate themselves from all their relatives and former associates who know of their background. This is essential if they wish to maintain contact with their family as then they must take great care to see that the right conditions are created whereby, they and their white associates never meet.

Crossing the Colour Line

Another good example of the difficulties involved in crossing the colour line in days of segregation in the USA is also given in *Black Metropolis.*

---

70 Drake and Clayton, *Black Metropolis*, 160.

My mother is very fair and passes for white on most of the jobs she has done, but she doesn't like to do it. It always brings about so much trouble. She makes friends, and soon they want her to come and see them, and they want to visit her. One friend that she had for over a year, used to invite mother to her apartment. This woman knew that mother had two children and she would say, 'You'll just have to bring those children over so that I can see them.' We would have fun talking about it. Well, she finally had to quit the job. The girl was becoming too chummy.

The final stage of passing – crossing over completely to the other side of the colour line – involves passing in order to associate socially with white people. For a Negro to pass socially, means sociological death and rebirth. It is extremely difficult, as one loses in the process his or her educational standing. If they have gone to a Negro school, intimate friends, family, work references are all affected. People well established in the Negro world and older people seldom pass socially or completely. There is too much to lose and too little to be gained.[71]

While conscious or unconscious passing for white undoubtedly did (and does) occur in the West Indies, there was neither the same drive behind the desire, nor the psychological tensions associated with it in Jamaica as there was in the southern states of the USA or in South Africa, where even the remotest connection with the Negro world could carry social ostracism. In former days it carried legal penalties for those who attempted to pass.

Colour in the West Indies

In the West Indies, back in Colonial days, in contrast to the USA, the very fair person of colour had no need to try to hide his or her ancestry, although normally they would be more ready to speak of their white heritage than of their links with the black world. They would say with simple pride that their grandfather was a Scotsman, or that their grandmother came from Dublin.

---

71   Drake and Clayton, *Black Metropolis*, 163.

The person who appeared white in the West Indies had nothing to fear, either from the law or from society where their position was accorded by appearance, rather than by genealogical investigation. It is further down the colour scale that psychological tensions were heightened and the desire to appear white or lighter was intensified.

The situation was complicated in British Guiana by intense interracial strife between the Indian and black sections of the population, further intensified by religious differences. To a lesser extent the same was true of Trinidad, while in Jamaica, the Chinese demonstrated their insularity in an otherwise completely multi-coloured and racially mixed society. Jamaica, however, was more typical of the rest of the British Caribbean than British Guiana.

White Bias

Jamaican society prior to independence, had as one of its main activating features, what we have termed a 'white bias'. This 'white bias' was dependent upon the practices and behaviour of individuals who were both consciously and unconsciously striving to 'lighten' themselves. In their minds 'black' was associated with the backward, primitive, and undesirable qualities in humanity, and 'white' was associated with everything that was desirable. This mindset was a direct derivation from colonial slavery which drove into the minds of African slaves in the Caribbean the enforced superiority of the white minority who held total power over their lives. That power was underwritten by law and enforced by the brutal application of punishment for any form of dissent.

Because of this inescapable colour heritage, the mind of the Jamaican was the seat of a deep conflict which was exhibited in the format of a particular personality configuration.

> The individual can have little pride of race in himself if he has the appearance of a coloured, or black man. At the same time, he has the perpetual desire to identify himself with the white man.[72]

This desire of the darker skinned man to enter the white man's world, was often only partially achieved, even by those in Government service, or by the wealthy. He could achieve a certain

---

72 Henriques, *Family and Colour in Jamaica*, 62.

degree of penetration into 'high society' but there would normally be a limit beyond which he was not expected to participate.

Where the position of a black man was such that he would expect to be admitted to social equality, as for example, that of a prominent Government official, we could speak of it as public acceptance by, or participation with, the fair group with whom he was in contact. That was to say, he would mix with fair people at a public function and be invited to semi-private entertainments in the home of fair people. For instance, he would be invited to attend a cocktail party given by the local Custos (the equivalent of the British 'Lord Lieutenant', or American State Governor). But he would never be invited to a party to which only close friends consisting of fair people had been invited.

Black Social Status

A black man would find it difficult to become a close friend of a fair person in the sense of an intimate relationship where each one enters freely each other's house. This tended to produce in black individuals a sense of hostility towards fair people and led to a kind of social isolation. They felt that black people were of an inferior economic status, were not sufficiently their friends, or equals, for them to become intimate.

Henriques, however, noted that there were ways in which the attitude of fair people could be rendered less rigid in terms of personal friendships. He said:

> Extreme wealth on the part of a black man is in itself comparatively rare. It will lead to a greater degree of acceptance. But of much greater advantage is the possession of a fair or white wife. Then the fair group feels that the wife must be accepted even at the cost of accepting the black husband. But the acceptance, achieved by whatever means, will never be the same as that extended to fair people, of similar economic position.[73]

Thus, in 1960s Jamaica where colour was inextricably bound up with the class system, the colour of one's skin was one of the determining factors governing social relationships. Colour even affected sex

73 Henriques, *Family and Colour in Jamaica*, 52.

relationships and marriage habits. A white or fair skinned man, in those days, would have his black or brown mistress, but it was most uncommon for him to marry her. He was much more likely to look for a wife amongst his own colour, or even fairer.

If he was a wealthy black man, or even a middle-class brown man, who wished to rise in the social scale, he had to enter a class of society not normally open to him. It was essential for him, therefore, to choose a wife fairer than himself.

Social Advantage

The middle or upper-class youth was instructed that a fair wife would greatly improve his chances of being economically and socially advantaged. The young woman was told that a husband not too much darker than herself would be a good match if his economic position was sound.

Another indication of 'white bias' was the practice amongst the well-to-do black or dark families, of having servants who were fair. This was done to emphasise to people that although dark, they exhibited superiority, to most dark people, and equality with fair people by employing the latter in a menial capacity. In Jamaica there were some outstanding cases, such as that of a wealthy black professional man in the capital who sent to England for a white governess for his daughter.[74]

Discrimination

Discrimination was not practised in Jamaican schools. Children of all colours and racial groups attended the same schools. But from an early age the child was able to see the disadvantages of being black as opposed to being fair or white. Suddenly a young black boy would realise that the fair boy would have the advantage of him in life. It may be an incident in the playground, or the way someone had spoken to him in the street – sometimes the realisation was enough to warp him for life. This, again, was part of the legacy of slavery with which people of colour had to learn to live if they were to survive in the world dominated by white superiority.

Teachers from England had been known to favour the white and fair children in Jamaica as against the black or dark child. The

---

74 Henriques, *Family and Colour in Jamaica,* 51.

school was the microcosm of the world of colour which awaited the individual outside. There were no rules to favour one group against another, but the approval given to the lighter coloured was as tacit as that given by society as a whole.

Fair coloured mothers would prevent their children from playing with black or dark children. On being questioned as to why they were doing this, the invariable answer was: 'I don't know where the black child may have come from.' There was some truth in this rationalisation, in that most black children did belong to a lower class, and so would be undesirable as playmates for a middle or upper-class child. But such a remark showed, and further indicated by general observation, that fair people associated all black people with the lower classes.

Indoctrination

If the child is not indoctrinated with prejudice by his or her parents, prior to going to school, he or she will mix perfectly well on equal terms with children of all colours until some other agency of colour education intervenes.

This was the finding of Bruce Lasker with regard to white and black children in the United States.[75] A similar view is expressed by Henriques, 'In the USA, as in Jamaica, the child is seldom allowed to develop a natural attitude towards colour without parental or school interference.'[76]

It is, of course, not easy to attempt, in the compass of a few pages, to try to summarise so difficult and complex a subject as colour and class attitudes in the West Indies as it was some 50 years ago. Such an attempt must inevitably be open to inaccuracies through generalisation, and in any case, as has already been indicated, the position was fluid owing to the changing political and economic forces at work in the Caribbean prior to the Independence of Jamaica in 1962.

The gap between the 1960s and the present day is bridged in Chapter 13 of this book by Alton Bell who brings the whole situation up to date by looking at the situation in Jamaica today.

---

75 Bruno Lasker, *Race in Children in New York*, 1929.
76 Filippo, *Family and Colour in Jamaica*, 57.

Chapter 12
DISCRIMINATION AND CHANGE

This is an important chapter for understanding historical roots of colour awareness with powerful examples drawn from the 1960s. It deals with the 'two worlds experience' of people of colour whom society classifies as black, but in their minds, they identify with the values of a white dominated society. This brings inevitable tensions which can be seen today.

Colour attitudes and discrimination are not easy subjects for research for the social investigator. A good start for the discussion of the subject occurs in *Jamaica, Land of Wood and Water* which although written in the 1960s is worth quoting as it gives an historical perspective.

Jamaica in the 1960s

Jamaicans as a rule, as has already been noted, avoid discussing the subject of discrimination with people of different colour groups. For example, a group of black professional men will inveigh against certain practices amongst themselves, but if a fair colleague were to join the group, the topic would be changed. Occasionally, colour prejudice will be discussed in the leader columns of newspapers, which will result in correspondence of the following kind.

The secretary of one of the islands' youth organisations wrote,

There seems to be a tendency in our country to avoid anything unpleasant as much as possible . . . But all this does not alter the fact that there is prejudice, and enough of it to kill much of the vigour, ambition, and enthusiasm, of many who would be the richest assets in the wonderful new Jamaica.'

A prominent black female Social Welfare worker wrote, from the black person's viewpoint:

I can tell a different tale. A tale of baffled, frustrated young people, especially women, who with sheaves of qualifications are unable to get a decent job outside the Government service. I have heard them through sheer economic necessity, decry the lack of wisdom and foresight of their parents in producing them the colour they are. I have seen them so filled with inferiority complex because of their black or, as they term it, dark colour, that they spend time and money on 'bleaching' so as to get away from themselves.

I have seen evidence of this colour prejudice wherever two or three are gathered. In schools, churches, in clubs, in societies of every sort. It affects us socially, politically, economically, and in every way. It is often the prejudice that exists between the varying shades of black and white and the black. It is the 'in-between' shades that are the cesspool of this evil . . .[77]

Colour Awareness

It is fairly obvious from all that has been said here that in the 1960s, West Indians of all colours were aware of colour distinctions and did much by their actions to perpetuate the system of colour gradings. The individual, of whatever group, was bound to become involved in discrimination, whatever his or her personal feelings may have been. Thus, although the natural choice for a brown man might have been a dark girl, there was sufficient family and social pressure to make him in the end choose a fairer girl.

We have already spoken of how family members would do everything to help the advancement of the fairest member. In the same way one's friends, associates, and acquaintances were chosen with this end in view. Of course, this particularly applied to the brown and fair groups, but as a general rule in the 1960s you associated with the people nearest to you in colour. We will see in the final chapter whether or not this is still relevant today.

Home Hospitality

While this rule could be broken from time to time in public, on particular occasions, it was rare for it not to be kept when it came to entertainment and hospitality in one's home. It was simply not

---

77 These quotes are all from personal correspondence with the author during a visit to Jamaica in 1962.

done for a brown family to entertain a black family. This is not to say that black and brown peasant families would have nothing to do with each other. But rather that middle classes of a dissimilar colour would not entertain each other in their homes. There was no compulsion about this. It was just something that was generally accepted. Association of black and brown could only be to the detriment of the brown. In any society which possesses distinctions of this kind, people will be anxious to maintain the position they have attained or attempt to improve it. Anything else would be regarded as a social disgrace.

To look at this somewhat crazy world of colour distinctions from as detached a position as possible, it seems obvious that the person who suffers most is the brown individual with 'good' (European) features and hair. The blacks can do very little about their position and thus are more resigned. The whites are secure and aloof in their whiteness. But the brown man is conscious that with perhaps a little alteration he might join the fair or the near white group. This consciousness must, surely, have an adverse effect upon his personality.

Living in Two Worlds

This colour consciousness shows itself in different ways. It is unsettling in terms of career or job, as well as in terms of personal relationships. The brown man is being pulled both ways. He knows that he is accepted as being superior to all those beneath him in the colour scale, yet he feels a certain affinity with them. On the other hand, he is aware of his inferiority vis-à-vis the fair and white groups and ardently desires to be identified with them. He is, in short, a man of two worlds which battle for the possession of his spirit.

But it would be wrong to assume that because the society was haunted by colour, the atmosphere was gloomy and full of animosity. Nothing could be farther from the truth. Jamaicans of all kinds back in the 1960s were known to be a happy people and there was far more spontaneous laughter and fun than in England. Superficially, there was little to indicate the depth of feeling on the subject of colour. It was only after a long period of staying that the visitor would become aware that little things which were thought a bit odd at the time, were part of a pervasive system. Jamaica in those early days of independence was a buoyant nation full of confidence for the future, and feelings about colour were undoubtedly changing at that time.

Universal Suffrage

A tremendous amount has been done since then in the creation of responsible government and universal suffrage. It has meant for the first time, in the history of the island, that black men have attained positions of power and authority. This has brought about their social acceptance publicly. It has also enhanced the prestige of the black people in the eyes of all Jamaicans. The old argument that only whites and near whites could do certain things is now almost dead. When black men appeared in the 'Government Appeal' it changed the social situation. Black and brown were working together in politics which opened the way for greater equality in other spheres of life, such as sport, especially cricket. But how far this has gone in changing the whole field of attitudes in society is questionable.

How did this work out for migrants?

From the traditional 'white bias' of a society dominated for centuries by a tiny European minority, the West Indian migrant came to Britain in the 'Windrush Generation' of the 1950s and 1960s. He had just begun to be subjected to the changing social patterns in his own island due to the demand for equality from the underprivileged sections of society and due to the political pressures at work behind the struggle for independence.

If he came from the rural districts of his native home, the migrant would have been less affected by the social forces which were making vast in-roads into the traditional structure of West Indian society, in the urban communities and in city life, as well as in government and the administrative services. Whether he came from a quiet country village, or a great commercial city, he would, to some extent have felt the 'winds of change' blowing upon his face, and bringing him faint but unmistakable tidings of a sweet freedom to be enjoyed and an emancipation from the burdens of 'colour'.

Racial Self-Consciousness

He would in some way have been caught up in the rising tide of racial self-consciousness that began sweeping through the world in the second half of the twentieth century and was gathering pace by the beginning of the 21st century. It is a tide which no one can stop; in which the black person has appeared publicly for the first time on the stage of history, in many spheres of life such as sport and entertainment, as well as politically, as a powerful force.

This tide was beginning to be seen as far back as the 1960s in the early days of independence in Jamaica, but it was also perceivable in Britain in open discussion on a national level of questions of colour and equality. In essence these were the issues underlying the debate in which Enoch Powell gained such prominence. The sheer numbers of black and coloured peoples in nations around the world could no longer be ignored – they had come to Britain not just as visitors, or on temporary work vouchers: they were marrying and creating families and becoming a settled part of the UK population. They could no longer be ignored or treated as second-class citizens.

Long before the end of the 20th century in Britain the demand for equality for black and people of colour had become irresistible. It was a tide in which black and the peoples of colour would accept nothing less than their just demands – the full rights and dignity of a common humanity, and an absolute and unreserved equality with the white man.

As far back as the 1960s I was seeing this and writing about it stating that if equality was not freely and willingly accorded by the white man – whether in Johannesburg South Africa, Birmingham Alabama USA, or Birmingham England – it would be taken by other means and the manner of its taking would be written into the history of the world by blood if necessary.

The World of 2020 and 'Black Lives Matter'

That final comment from the 1960s, that the day would come when 'black people and people of colour will accept nothing less than their just demands – the full rights and dignity of a common humanity' was surely a prophetic statement that is coming true today. The campaign that sprang to life during the pandemic worldwide lockdown period in May 2020, not only showed the pent-up passion and frustration of black and brown people, but it was an indication that their just demands were at last being heard by people of many nations across the world.

Many people of all colours and racial distinctions responded warmly to the 'Black Lives Matter' protest movement demanding greater efforts from the authorities to ensure their fair treatment at the hands of police and wider recognition of the demands for equality in all walks of life.

Like all such protests, it attracted those who had wider political agendas, as has happened with other 'single issue topics' like climate change. In 2019, climate-control protesters glued themselves to the roads in order to disrupt traffic in London and to make the maximum impact of their activities. Anarchist groups also joined the street protests against parliamentary proposals to tighten the laws on policing public demonstrations under the title 'Kill the Bill'.

Many people discerned the objectives of these groups and sounded warnings sufficiently strongly for the movements to lose momentum. Any immediate danger of revolution was avoided, but how this will affect the movement for justice and equality in matters of race and colour has yet to be seen.

Chapter 13

COLOUR CONSCIOUSNESS IN THE CARIBBEAN

THE COLONIAL PIGMENTOCRATIC SYSTEM

In this chapter Alton Bell continues the theme of colour consciousness and investigates its origins and the extent to which it has spread across the world. He writes both academically and from the personal standpoint of a man of colour living in a white man's world which makes his observations particularly penetrating.

In the 18th century, as we have seen, individuals were categorised by skin colour and degrees of whiteness. The categories were: black, mulatto, terceroon, quadroon, mustee, musteefino and white. The child of a white person and a Mustee, Musteefino or Quadroon was regarded as English. Lightness, valued as a promise of higher status, became valued for itself, and status was equated with lightness. The same social hierarchy based on skin tone that characterised Jamaican life during enslavement also operated during the emancipation period.

Social Class and Wealth

Colonialism was built on class and money. The more money you had the higher up the pecking order you could ascend. However, on the plantations where all the wealth was generated, classism was underpinned by a complex pigmentocratic colour system which located people in the hierarchy. Their position in society was based on skin tone which was extremely complex and used to describe the system of privilege and discrimination based on the degree of lightness in the colour of a person's skin. In Jamaica it is still common today to refer to people by nicknames given according to their skin tone. For example, my uncle was called 'lighty' and it was not until he died that I discovered this was not his real name. Today, people are still referred to by names such as: 'blacks', 'reds', 'lighty', 'blacka' and so on without recourse to their historical antecedents.

Colour Labels

Colourism, and shadism are labels used to describe the colour system. However, whatever terms are used to describe it, it remains a pernicious, internalised form of racism which involves prejudice, stereotyping and perceptions of beauty among members of the same racial group. In this system light skin is more highly valued than dark skin. It is important to note that colourism is a product of white supremacy and racism which did not exist or evolve independently.

It could be argued that racism is the building block of colourism and the reverse is also true that colourism is the building block of racism. The two are interwoven in society in many parts of the Western world. White supremacy is often associated with overt displays of racism from certain groups such as neo-Nazi extremists and the Ku Klux Klan.

A succinct definition of society where racism exists is : 'White supremacy is the sea that the western world swims in.' It expresses itself as the routine privileging of white interests that goes un-remarked in the political mainstream. This is both structured in domination and represents a form of tacit intentionality on the part of white power holders and policymakers. White privilege occurs because of white supremacy through a process which places a higher value on the lighter skin colour.

Colonialism

Europeans who colonised the Americas were involved in the dehumanisation of those from Africa, by reducing them to the status of chattel (treating them as cattle) for economic exploitation. This brought about a profound change in human relations. The standard for a human, or the figure of a whole person, was now the white supremacist, who was the patriarchal, capitalist figure, with everyone else subservient.

The Transatlantic Slave Trade is generally regarded as a defining period in history, in terms of establishing the foundations of the systematic and globalized domination of African peoples and the perpetuation of ideologies which claimed white superiority. In describing an encounter between Africans and Europeans in the 16th century, the historian Jordan[78] remarked that Europeans were struck by the colour of the African's skin; and thereafter whenever a traveller referred to Africans, they always mention their colour.

Black and White

However, well before the encounter with Africans in the sixteenth century, the English had already assigned a variety of negative aesthetic and moral values to the word 'black'. To be black was to be dirty, ugly, evil, deadly, devilish. To be white was to be clean, beautiful, good, lively, and godly. Blackness acquired negative connotations in the European psyche as early as the 3rd century CE, through the writings of the early Christian Fathers who depicted blackness as being synonymous with sin.

The theme of darkness was introduced as the antithesis of spiritual light by Origen, head of the catechetical school in Alexandria. Initially the theme of darkness had nothing to do with skin colour, but over time became associated with racial representations. Early Medieval paintings often depicted black devils as Christ's tormentors during the Passion. Religious folklore is littered with negative connotations of blackness from stories of sin turning men black, to stories of black people being born in hell, to tales of Ormazd and Ahriman in Zoroastrianism – Children of Light and Children of Darkness.

According to Greek legend, Phaeton's chariot drew the sun too close to the earth, resulting in the blackening of the faces of the Ethiopians. Biological differences between Blacks and Whites have been used historically as a justification for imposing negative values on people of colour, which in turn are used to justify the subjugation, oppression and economic domination of so-called inferior races by white hegemonies.

The Theological Justification for Enslavement of Africans

In the 6th century, the myth of the curse of Ham, a son of Noah, was created by European rabbis and Talmudists. Ham was regarded

---

78   As quoted in M.V. Adams, *The Multicultural Imagination: Race, Colour and the Unconscious*, Routledge, London 1996, 20. see also W.D. Jordan, *American Chiaroscuro: The Status and Definition of Mulattos in the British Colonies*, The William and Mary Quarterly, 3rd Edn., Vol. 19, No. 2 (April 1962), 183-200.

as progenitor of the black race. In Genesis 9:22-25 in the Old Testament, after the flood had taken place, Noah falls into a drunken stupor and is naked in his tent. When Ham discovers him, he tells his brothers Shem and Japheth, who bring a cloak and cover Noah's body, being careful not to look at his nakedness. When Noah sobers up, he discovers what Ham did, and scolds him, and pronounces a curse over his grandson Canaan. This is what he says: '**Cursed be Canaan, slave of slaves, shall he be to his brothers.**' There is no mention of skin colour in the narrative.

The Talmud

But in the Jewish version of Genesis 9:25-27 in the Babylonian Talmud, Noah says:

> Now I cannot beget the fourth son whose children I would have ordered to serve you and your brothers. Therefore, it must be Canaan, your first born, whom they enslave. And since you have disabled me . . . doing ugly things in blackness of night, Canaan's children shall be born ugly and black!

The Talmudic version also suggests that African facial features are a curse from Noah, along with oversized sexual organs:

> Because you twisted your head around to see my nakedness, your grandchildren's hair shall be twisted into kinks and their eyes red; again, because your lips jested at my misfortune, theirs shall swell, their male members shall be shamefully elongated! Men of this race are called Negros.[79]

During the Middle Ages the European representation of the world depicted the three sons of Noah as progenitors of the European, African, and Asian continents. In 1442, Pope Eugenius IV issued a papal bull or decree – *Illius Qui* – which approved of Portugal's Prince Henry's slave trading expeditions to Africa and then gave Portugal sole rights over all its discoveries.[80]

His successor, Pope Nicholas V issued another Bull, Romanus Pontifex in January 1454, which gave formal support to Portugal's

---

79   See J. Ben-Jochannan, *The Myth of Exodus and Genesis and the Exclusion of their African Origins*, Black Classic Press, Baltimore 1996, 17.

80   Hugh Thomas, *The Slave Trade: The story of the Atlantic Slave Trade, 1440-1870*, Touchstone books, 1997, 64-65.

monopoly of trading in Africa, which included Africans, as well as the instruction to convert them to the Christian faith. This Bull was read out in the Cathedral of Lisbon in both Latin and Portuguese, and as one historian pointed out, it helped to establish the familiar Portuguese pattern of 'making money', 'saving' Africans from 'barbarism', the excitement of voyages down the Guinea coast and raiding expeditions up the rivers.'[81]

The Portuguese enslaved Africans and took them to Portugal. The slave markets in Lagos became the place where the newly baptised Africans were bought by merchants and traders to labour in a range of establishments. Many were put to work in the cultivation of sugarcane on the Portuguese island of Madeira, and this combination of sugar and slave labour was subsequently exported to the Caribbean by Columbus and his successors.

Slave Castles

In 1482, the Portuguese built the infamous Elmina Castle in what is modern-day Ghana, which was used as the primary means of protecting their possessions in that part of West Africa. In time, the castle became infamous as the place where enslaved Africans were held over centuries.[82] Much like the Cape Coast Castle, also in Ghana, both edifices had chapels. In the Cape Coast Castle, the chapel was constructed directly above the male slave dungeon, which meant that the Africans could hear their white Christian captors singing as they languished in their hell-like conditions.

Over time, these castles would change ownership due to European rivalries over Africa, but irrespective of whether they were in Portuguese, Dutch, or in British hands, the churches would have clergy who cared for the spiritual welfare of the Europeans stationed there.

European Dominance

In 1593, the production of Iconologia, a book of emblems by Cesare Ripa, portrayed Europe as a Queen with a crown and golden rod, Asia as a woman adorned with gold jewellery carrying spices

---

81 Thomas, *The Slave Trade*, 65.

82 James Pope-Hennessy, *Sins of the Father: The Atlantic Slave Traders – 1441 -1807*, Phoenix Press.2000, 55-60.

and incense and Africa as an almost naked woman carrying an elephant's trunk. In the 16th century after Europeans 'discovered' America, it was added as the fourth continent.[83]

Early 2nd century and 4th century BCE biblical writings that make reference to Shem, Ham and Japheth have no links to the continents of Africa, Asia and Europe, as those links did not exist then. This racial and geographical connection was invented by Flavius Josephus, a Hellenized Jew towards the end of the first century of the Christian era. The construction of European representations of the world placed Europe at the centre of the universe, and other continents and races as subordinates.

The Jewish version of the curse of Ham became popular among Christians in the 16th century, around the time that Europeans began their invasion of the African continent and the chattel enslavement of African peoples. Rudolph Windsor in his study of the history of ancient black races, states that in ancient times blacks did not classify races according to skin colour.[84] But clan names were the means by which individuals were identified.

New Mixed Class

We must be aware that although Europeans are primarily associated with structural and systemized forms of racial domination in the 21st century, there are scholars who remind us that colourism occurred in Africa well before the invasion of the Europeans. In his writings, Dr Chancellor Williams alludes to colourism and its role in the ethnic transformation of Egypt, which once formed the north-eastern region of ancient Ethiopia.[85] As a result of relentless conquests, Asians came to occupy a quarter of Egypt in the 3rd millennium BCE. The intermixing between Africans and Asians produced a new mixed class, but in the new imposed social order, black Africans (the darkest Egyptians) were pushed to

---

83 Deborah Gabriel, *Layers of Blackness: Colourism in the African Diaspora*, Imani Media Limited, 2007, 8.

84 Rudolph Windsor, *From Babylon to Timbuktu: A History of Ancient Black Races Including the Black Hebrews,* 20th edn., Windsor's Golden Series, Atlanta 2003.

85 C. Williams, *The Destruction of Black Civilisation: Great Issues of a Race from 4500 B.C. to 2000 A.D.*, Third World Press, Chicago 1987.

the bottom of the social, economic, and political ladder wherever the Asians and their mulatto offspring gained control.

The collusion between church and state was embellished by science to create a system of white supremacy. This is the system that is being challenged across the globe with the rise of the Black Lives Matter movement, after the very graphic and heinous killing of George Floyd under the knee of a white law enforcement officer in Minneapolis, USA in May 2020. After centuries of agitation for social justice by activists, the systems and structures built on false theories of a racial superiority are beginning to shake. The year 2020 was very significant and the global pandemic added to that urgency.

Freedom Soon?!

Manumission did not occur on a frequent basis in the British Caribbean, but when it did, it was usually in favour of mulatto concubines and mulatto children who were often provided with an education. In the latter part of the 18th century, many white slave owners left Jamaica for England to live in luxury off the wealth created from enslaved Africans. However, when the revenue from the plantations declined and plantation owners began to sink into debt, many more left the colonies. The movement off the island by the Whites left a void in the social hierarchy, which was filled by Mulattos, the majority of whom were offspring of the plantation owners and their concubines. It is important to note that many had been educated in the UK.

The protection of the offspring of Whites was written into the original colonial charters, which gave certain privileges to Mulattos, such as a higher social status than dark-skinned Blacks. Concubinage in Jamaica was not only sanctioned, but almost encouraged. The historian Edward Long, wrote in Volume II of The History of Jamaica:

> He who should presume to shew any displeasure against such a thing as simple fornication, would for his pains be accounted a simple blockhead; since not one in twenty can be persuaded, that there is either sin; or shame in cohabiting with his slave.[86]

---

86 Edward Long, *History of Jamaica*, Cambridge University Press, Cambridge 2010.

Rise of Mulattos

Many Mulattos inherited property from their white ancestors, sometimes when there were no legitimate heirs to white estates: as illegitimate heirs, they were granted an inheritance and began to acquire great wealth.

Mulattos entered the professions, trades, and administrative jobs mostly in urban areas and before apprenticeships began. They made up the majority of voters in Kingston and the three surrounding Parishes. After the decline of the planter class, the roles of Mulattos increased. Many became educated, acquired property in urban areas and inter-married.

John Bigelow, owner and editor of the *New York Post*, reported after a visit to Jamaica in 1850, that both revenue officers and the majority of police officers were Mulattos. Inter-marriage was a common feature between Whites and Mulattos, whose families regularly moved in the same social circles. In the middle of the twentieth century illiteracy rates for children of seven years and older stood at 98.6 per cent for blacks, compared with 88.9 per cent for Mulattos, 87.5 for Chinese, 97.7 for East Indians and 38.8 per cent for Whites. Surveys carried out in 1950 and 1951 into the complexion of professional doctors and lawyers, found that a large portion was light skinned: those 'who by the attainment of professional status have validated an elite identity.'[87]

It should be noted that despite the distinctions made between dark-skinned Blacks and Mulattos, which had served to foster divisions between the two groups, after the Abolition of the Slave Trade in 1807, Mulattos were not granted full citizenship rights, although many of them owned and ran the Islands plantations. Like their darker skinned 'colleagues' they were prohibited from giving evidence against a white person and were denied the right to vote. They petitioned the Jamaica Assembly in 1823 asking for the removal of restrictions on their citizenship rights, but the Jamaican Assembly refused.

Three years later Jews were granted full rights, but Mulattos continued to be denied. After this point they joined with the rest of the black population to bolster their cause. The passing of the Emancipation Act in 1833 led to the abolition of Slavery in the British

---

87 Broom, L, 'The Social Differentiation in Jamaica', American Sociological Review, Vol. 19, No. 2, April 1954, p.115-125.

Colonies; however, this represented partial freedom as all ex-slaves and Mulattos had to carry their manumission papers with them wherever they went.

Colourism Today

Full emancipation occurred in 1838 after the British Parliament voted to compensate the slavers to the tune of £20m, but gave the ex-slaves not a single penny, as noted elsewhere in this book. For me as a Jamaican, this is particularly significant as I grew up in a rural community that had inherited the problems created by the terms of the 1833 emancipation. However, class distinctions based upon skin colour have been hard to eradicate. And the notion that anything or anyone too black is somehow not good, is still prevalent in the psyche of most Jamaicans. Post-Traumatic Slave Syndrome (PTSS)[88] and Acquired Anti-Own Race Syndrome (AAORS – see next page) are hard to eradicate.

When Jamaica gained independence from the British Empire in 1962, it merely represented the transfer of power from the white colonial elite to the local black bourgeoisie. However, economic power remained with the local white settler class and a large proportion of Mulattos. As a result of this legacy, Jamaican society is characterised by a 'struggle' between 'middle' and 'upper-class' British-educated Jamaicans who subscribe to the 'superiority' of British culture and . . . a people's culture whose defiance of the 'super-culture' is expressed most artfully in the reggae music of Bob Marley, Jimmy Cliff and Don Drummond.[89]

White Superiority

Marcus Garvey lamented in 1916, that despite 78 years having passed since emancipation, Jamaica had not managed to produce a credible black leader. In a letter he wrote that year to Booker T. Washington's successor at the Tuskegee Institute, Garvey shared his concerns about the widespread impact of colourism on Jamaican society:

---

88 This term was coined by sociologist Dr Joy Degruy in her 1995 thesis on the legacy of trauma from slavery in America.

89 B.D. Headley, 'Toward a Cyclical Theory of Race Relations in Jamaica', *Journal of Black Studies*, Vol. 15, No. 2, Dec. 1984, 207-222.

The whites claim superiority, as is done all over the world, and, unlike other parts, the coloured, who ancestrally are the illegitimate off-springs of black and white, claim a positive superiority over the blacks. They train themselves to believe that in the slightest shade, the coloured man is above the black man and so it runs right up to white . . .

Like John Bigelow 66 years earlier, Garvey observed that Mulattos dominated the administrative and professional occupations. To Garvey, Blacks in Jamaica inherited a damaged psychology as a result of being enslaved and colonised by Whites, which resulted in the self-negation of black identity and black interests:

Whenever a black man enters the professions, he per force, thinks from a white and coloured mind . . . Whenever the black man gets money and education, he thinks himself white and coloured, and he wants a white and coloured wife, and he will spend his all to get this; much to his eternal misery.[90]

Legacy of Slavery

Contemporary scholars have observed, like Garvey, that one of the most damaging legacies of slavery was its impact on the psyche of Jamaican people. This is often manifested through a condition called **Acquired Anti-Own Race Syndrome** (AAORS), which is defined as:

The philosophy and psychology of assumed European world cultural superiority expressed by African peoples in their relations with each other and in perceiving and operating in the world.[91]

It is characterised by self-denial and self-negation factors associated with colourism.

In that same article, Clinton Hutton, a lecturer in political philosophy and culture at the University of the West Indies in Mona, alludes to a novel by Alice Spinner published in 1984 called *A Study in Colour*, in which the characters were real people interviewed by

---

90 C.S. Matthew, 'Marcus Garvey Writes from Jamaica on the Mulatto Escape Hatch', *Journal of Negro History,* Vol 59, No. 2, April 1974, 170-176.

91 Clinton Hutton, *Acquired Anti-Own Race Syndrome*, African Peoples Review of Anthropology, Vol. 33, Oct 2004, 583-623.

the author. One of these characters, Justina, spoke of her desire for a light skinned child as opposed to a dark-skinned child, who she felt would 'bring shame on her,' She confessed that she could not find it in her heart to love a dark-skinned child and revealed her ambition to marry a light-skinned man to improve her social status.

Feminine Beauty

It is, however, not just skin tone that colour-conscious Jamaicans are obsessed with. 'Texture and length of hair are linked to the racist notion of femininity and feminine beauty.' AAORS (and by association colourism) have a negative impact on Jamaican society because of the disunity it fosters amongst black people.

There is no greater sin of slavery than the systematic brain washing that occurred for over 300 years that instilled a belief in the second-class character of the people of African descent. This distorted image received by people of African descent continues to haunt their psyche today as an enduring sin of slavery.

Chapter 14

THE COLOUR CODE AND STATUS DISTINCTIONS:

AN INCURABLE DISEASE?

In this chapter Nigel Pocock deals with the subject of colour consciousness from a psychosomatic standpoint, particularly looking at the psychological effect upon the health of individuals with their different experience of racial prejudice. He examines different concepts of social change and offers some practical steps towards overcoming the entrenched colour code differentiation in the Caribbean that is part of the legacy of colonial slavery. **At the close, he outlines aspects of the Christian message which motivates individuals to change.**[92]

> *Again, I saw all the oppressions that are practiced under the sun. And behold, the tears of the oppressed, and they had no one to comfort them! On the side of their oppressors there was power, and there was no one to comfort them. And I thought that the dead who are already dead are more fortunate than the living who are still alive; but better than both is he who has not yet been born, and not yet seen the evil deeds that are done under the sun. Then I saw that all toil and all skill in work come from man's envy of his neighbour.*
>
> Ecclesiastes 4:1-4

Light vs. Darkness: the Problem Facing Us All

There is nothing new under the sun, as Ecclesiastes 1.9 quoted above also reminds us. As long as people have been on earth, disease and war have also prevailed. Why should things be any

---

92   William Hasker, *The Triumph of God Over Evil,* IVP, Downers Grove, IL 2008, 90ff., addresses psychological determinism, and the importance of what is a person's strongest motivation.

different now? Since Cain murdered his brother Abel (Genesis 4:8) violence has characterised human relationships. Human beings have a propensity towards aggression in defence of their territory or personal rights. The whole of human history substantiates this statement. Sadly, human beings do not seem to be learning from the past and the twentieth century, with its two world wars and the central European Holocaust with the murder of more than six million Jews. **Stalin's, Mao's and Pol Pot's misguided atrocities** saw **possibly the shedding of more blood than at any other time in recorded history.**[93] **As psychiatrist Anthony Storr put it, humans are the most violent species that has ever walked the earth.**

Alas, both good and evil are in the hearts of men and women – altruistic towards their kith and kin, defensive towards anything that threatens their sacred space. Both are necessary, it would seem, for the survival of the species. What then drives human violence? Is it fear, as activist Jim Wallis suggests?[94] Commensurate with fear, an absence of truth, for men and women often prefer darkness, rather than light, lest their evil deeds should be exposed, as Jesus said: *"This is the verdict: light has come into the world, but men loved darkness instead of light because their deeds were evil"* (John 3:19), a theme developed in John's First Letter.

Is there any reason to think that people have become more compassionate and pro-social since the time of Jesus some 2000 years ago? Is it true that people are walking a path towards ever-increasing goodness, as Idealists would like us to believe? Has the destruction of people and family, under colonial slavery that we have been examining in this book, any lessons for us today?

The Importance of Values

In this chapter we are going to suggest that while changes to society and culture should be made, there are always dark forces waiting in the wings. People have all kinds of motives for their behaviour. They are not blank slates, onto which goodness can simply be inscribed, but they have brains with developed

---

93 See the *Guinness Book of Records* for a comparison of various genocides, going back to Genghis Khan to the present day.

94 Jim Wallis (2019). *Christ in Crisis: Reclaiming Jesus*, HarperCollins, London, Chapter 6.

structures for such things as language,[95] including the language of colour-coding.

From infancy, children have neural structures that facilitate the rapid acquisition of speech, and in this way the culture is transmitted from one generation to the next. It is the culture of values, including racial and tribal values, that shape the expression of language. People are profoundly impacted by a thousand variables, which interact dynamically to produce the culture of a nation.

Active in What we Know

Human beings define themselves through their actions, not just morally, but psychologically and neurologically, in the relationship between action and attitude. Each informs and shapes the other.[96] For example: any planter who is a racist becomes even more of a ruthless planter and racist, the more they practise their violent activities. Their actions become the norm and form the culture that legitimises their actions and attitudes. That was the situation that developed during the 300 **or more** years of colonial slavery. It became a culture embedded in the life of the nations in the West Indian territories.

These social values are not irrational, for they represent attempts to legitimate certain specific cultural and personal goals. The colour-code and pigmentocracy were a means to establish the power and supposed legitimacy of a dominant group, over/against others. It was designed to maintain this power and its privileges. If we are to address such culturally-legitimated violence, then we need to be committed to truth, and be unafraid to bring evil deeds into the light, without fear. It means exposing injustice however well-established and embedded in the accepted culture of a nation.

Facing the Truth is Essential

The Black Lives Matter campaign brought racial injustice to public attention following the highly publicised murder of George Floyd by a white policeman in Minneapolis. But exposing the existence of injustice by actions such as taking the knee at a football match, does not banish the injustice, because those who hold different

---

95   Steven Pinker, *The Blank Slate*, Penguin, London 2002..
96   David G. Myers in *Psychology*, Vol. 4, Worth, New York 1995.

viewpoints justify them by appealing to a different set of values, and even by holding a different memory of the past.

This calls for both maturity[97] and openness to truth.[98] As Scott Peck has observed, it is in an 'ongoing dedication to reality at all costs' that good mental health is found, black and white, shame notwithstanding.[99] Colour-coding immediately suggests a certain polarisation in community relationships, which needs to be tackled at its roots.

In an interesting article on social polarisation in the 2020 Trump-Biden US election, Matthew Patrick Riley makes some helpful observations that are relevant to the divided world of black and white relationships.[100] He starts by observing that Americans lack a **shared** historical memory. Black and white each remember the past differently. This contributes to social polarisation. Their different memories of the past, lead to strongly held, **and differing** viewpoints.

Polarised Groups

For whom was President Trump aiming to 'make America great again' (MAGA)? Was it for the benefit of Whites, or African-Americans? Supporters of MAGA recall abolition and are in denial about specifically Christian legitimations for slavery. By contrast the 'lament' group stress the negative fallouts from the past: land theft, slavery, abuse of women, police brutality and oppression. The past is not past. It is still very much the present.

The 'make better' group focuses on avoiding both excessive praise and criticisms. For them, a more balanced and nuanced understanding of the past is **what is** appropriate. As psychologist Roy Baumeister has pointed out, both perpetrators and victims skew their

---

97   J. D. Carter, 'Maturity, Psychological and Biblical', in H. Newton Malony (ed.), *Wholeness and Holiness: Readings in the Psychology/Theology of Mental Health*, Baker, Michigan 1993, 184-193.

98   C. Daniel Batson, 'Patricia Schoenrade' in W. Larry Ventis, *Religion and the Individual*, Oxford University Press, Oxford 1993, 238-239.

99   M. Scott Peck, *Further Along the Road Less Travelled*, Simon & Schuster, London 1993, 75.

100   Matthew Patrick Riley, 'From Make America Great Again to Make America Better: How US History Shapes Christianity and Politics', *The Conversation*, University College, London 20th November 2020. Matthew Patrick Riley is an Honorary Visiting Fellow, University of Leicester.

understandings of the past, when compared to a neutral observer. Victims make an event seem worse than it was, while perpetrators play it down, or deny it altogether. Both groups have self-defined identity needs, and these find expression in their views of reality and history. But both present a selective picture of the truth. Victims may see things in terms of gross injustice, while perpetrators see circumstances that gave them a justification for their actions.[101]

Facing the Past — Constructive Criticism

What then is to be done? Both MAGA and 'lament' are too skewed to achieve harmony. Thus, there is a need for a bridge that will break down the polarised understanding of history. The drive to achieve justice and equality needs to be a bipartisan effort. Thus the 'better' position is that it shows how criticism can be a sign of constructive loyalty to the country, not the reverse. It represents a call for *maturity,* defined as not retreating into denial, but facing reality. As Rowley writes, 'a nation has come of age when it can squarely face its past'. This is surely right. Slavery corrupted everybody, black, white, and brown, as the slave narratives make clear.[102]

Maturity

It is to this call for maturity that we now turn. Other important characteristics of maturity lie in not denying the past but being flexible and not blaming others for our own mistakes; forgiving others, being both reflective, and yet able to appreciate and enjoy the company of others in a way that is culturally appropriate. This is the narrative that both MAGA (perhaps as 'Make Africa Great Again!') and 'lament' need to arrive at in the USA, in order to find a creative and peaceful way forward.

We can already see much that suggests a way forward in terms of acceptance of different cultures throughout the Western world. Examples can be seen in the increasing appearance of African hairstyles in the fashion industry and people of colour being seen in the media and becoming numbered among celebrities in sport

---

101   Roy Baumeister, *Evil: Inside Human Violence and Cruelty*, Barnes & Noble, New York 1997, 46-47.

102   Yuval Taylor, *I Was Born a Slave: An Anthology of Classic Slave Narratives*, 2 Vols., Canongate, Edinburgh 1999.

and entertainment. Their successes are heralded alongside those of white people on the basis of complete equality and acceptance, without it being remarkable. This is the kind of acceptance that is needed as a step towards full equality.

Meritocracy Increases Stresses

Meritocracy introduces further conflict, for, as de Botton[103] notes, it means that people can no longer blame the system, but only themselves. They have nowhere to go, particularly if hereditable effects are denied – and it may be that achievement is at least 50% or more due to hereditable effects on the genes, over time.[104] This is the conflict for some brown people, caught in opposing currents, being neither black African, nor white (at least in appearance), but aspiring to be fair-skinned, because of the status this implies, all driven by status anxiety.

Today, to be called an 'Oreo' (black outside, white inside, and other variants) is an insult and a term of abuse.[105] [106] In order to develop the maturity needed to address the colour code and its mental, physical, and social pathologies, the hereditable elements, if they reduce ability to achieve, must be recognised. Only then, with recognition, can these disadvantages be addressed.

Causes Must be Addressed

The colour code is both a social and structural disease originating in slavery. It spawns personal trauma and 'self-racism', an internalised attitude that increases trauma because it perpetuates injustice between the varying degrees of skin colour. To treat the one-to-one effects of this trauma may be counter-productive for society (while being very important to the victim, and their immediate family) since it avoids addressing the larger causes rather than the historically conditioned origins. Counselling simply helps people to cope with

---

103   Alain de Botton, *Status Anxiety*, Penguin, London 2005, 86.

104   Pinker, *The Blank Slate*.

105   Kai Morgan and Keisha-Gaye N. O'Garo, 'Caribbean Identity Issues', in Frederick W. Hickling, Brigitte Matties, Kai Morgan, Roger C. Gibson (eds.), *Perspectives in Caribbean Psychology*, Jessica Kingsley, London 2012, 27.

106   Frederick W. Hickling, 'Psychopathology of the Jamaican People', in Hickling *et al.*, *Perspectives in Caribbean Psychology*, 37-38.

the effects of the colour code, so it does nothing to combat social discrimination in society – in fact, it could be argued that it reinforces it, by enabling people to live with it, rather than changing it.

Counselling may Actually be Dysfunctional

Psychologists know that happy people, and psychologically mature people, have goals in life that are both long-term and for the good of society, and that the colour code, being fundamentally unjust, must lead to unhappiness. Psychiatrist Raj Persaud writes:

Counsellors help people to deal with the effects of many questionable state policies, thus *diverting attention away from the political, social, and economic causes of distress*. For example, counselling treatment programmes were developed for black refugees in South African townships who suffered from policies of apartheid and police brutality.

According to economic theorists, widespread human misery is inescapable within societies which ordain particular power relations between people. The issue then sometimes becomes whether we want to work to change ourselves, or to change society. The danger of *counselling is that it obfuscates this issue.*[107]

Helping Others to Find Healing

Political, social, and economic reforms are largely responsible for improving relations between people, not personal counselling. Personal counselling creates a conflict between mental contentedness and altruism because mental health is achieved through introspection, not social action. People become inward-looking rather than finding contentment from their actions in the world in order to change the value system for the benefit of the whole of humanity.

Those who suffer injustice due to the colour code should ideally find healing, not in personal counselling to deal with their own trauma, but in action to promote a change in the value system of society, to bring healing to multitudes who suffer from similar injustice. The victim, in finding personal healing, finds a *moral* principle that is bigger than themselves and which represents much

---

107   Raj Persaud (1997). *Staying Sane*, London, Metro.

more substantial social needs than himself/herself, and therefore the whole community, black, brown, and white, benefits.

Speaking out in public reinforces this healing which walks hand-in-hand with increasing psychological maturity. Part of this maturation lies in the recognition that not every battle will be won. The mark of the mature person is an ability to face life realistically. Working with others, even in defeat, increases social capital (particularly an attitude of humility, honesty, and mutual fellowship) over a range of persons and situations. Increased social capital, leads to increased happiness and contentedness for society as a whole.

Harsh Discipline and Fixed Mindsets

Surveys in the Caribbean show that not only is there a long tradition of harsh discipline in home, school, and general culture, but that people from young to old continue to support and endorse this culture of physical discipline.[108] This is likely to be a part of a closed mindset, in which there are poor problem-solving skills, with knee-jerk answers.[109] Where a problem is too challenging, facing it is avoided, no matter to what level of education the person might be.[110]

Changing attitudes towards the use of physical discipline which was an integral part of colonial slavery could be an important first step in changing attitudes towards colour code discrimination in the Caribbean. It would be taking an important step away from the mindset of slavery into a new sense of freedom and identity. By definition, a well-educated person is one who has learned to face, accept, and constructively utilise criticism. This is the 'growth mindset' that leaves behind the old mindset of slavery that enforces discipline externally rather than embraces it individually as a personal choice. This could provide an important step towards tackling the insidious colour code discrimination that is deeply institutionalised in Caribbean culture which is part of the legacy of slavery.

---

108   Brigitte K. Matthies, Julie Meeks-Gardner, Avril Daley, Claudette Crawford-Brown, 'Issues of Violence in the Caribbean', in Hickling *et al.*, *Perspectives in Caribbean Psychology*, 393 ff.

109   Milton Rokeach, *The Open and Closed Mind*, Basic Books, New York 1960.

110   Carol Dweck, *Mindset*, Robinson, London 2012, gives many examples of this.

Achieving Change: Not Too Quickly?

E. M. Rogers and F. F. Shoemaker produced a helpful model to describe the rate of social change in a group. They suggest

- Innovators — 2.5% of the group introduce the new ideas

- Early adopters — 13.5% welcome the changes and promote them

- Early majority — 34% (total 50%) who had/have reservations, but now accept and promote the changes, making a majority of the group

- Late majority — 34% who were resistant, but have been won over by group C

- Laggards — 16% who accept the changes grudgingly. They were ready to leave, and will continue to resist, even when the changes have themselves become traditional.[111]

These are, of course, no more than a general pattern, but a useful predictor of what might be expected on the introduction of factors of change. However, if change is introduced with a speed with which the group cannot cope, then fragmentation will occur. Wearing down deeply-held prejudices such as colour coding will probably take a great deal of time and effort – decades rather than years.

The Adoption of Change

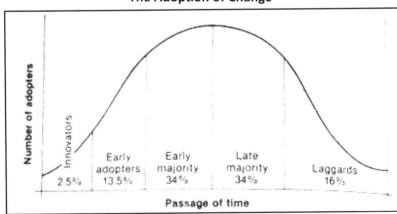

---

111 Cited by Roy Pointer, *How Do Churches Grow?* MARC Europe, London 1984, 57-8.

The adoption of change—too fast!

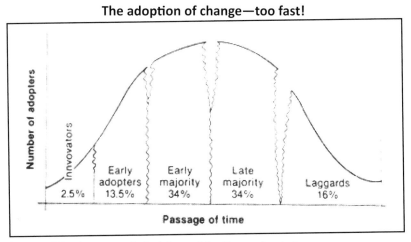

Some Modest and Achievable Practical Steps

From a Christian perspective, what is needed is a form of 'realised eschatology'.[112] Christians need to be a prophetic people working towards the realisation of a just society, putting into practice the biblical principles of justice and equality that are the foundations of a just society. Those who are not familiar with the Bible may not realise that the nature of God is revealed as being: justice, love, compassion, faithfulness, and integrity. God is shown as the God of creation who made all human beings equal, with no distinctions of race, gender, or nationality. He is also shown to be a God who hates violence and condemns the shedding of innocent blood, and who desires all human beings to live in peace and harmony, caring for each other and working together for the common good.

To make this potentially achievable, several modest steps are required:

- A definition of biblical truth
- A practical tool for the realisation of this vision
- Political will and vision
- A practical application to colour coding, for example using Brigitte Matthies' 5 steps (*next page*)[113]

---

112 'Realised Eschatology' is a theological concept by which a future vision becomes a present reality. It is actually living today in what will only become fully realised in some future age.

113 Brigitte Matthies is Assistant Professor, Department of Psychology, California State University, Los Angles.

These steps do not need to be addressed in this chronological order. They can start at any point and run concurrently. We will start with Brigitte Matthies' 'General Recommendations' regarding violence in the Caribbean, as they are directly applicable to the issue of colour-coding as a system designed to be unfair and unjust to any group 'beneath' it.[114] The steps are as follows:

1 Reform and strengthening of legal, judicial, and policing systems. This should involve the community in monitoring and education. Regarding any unfairness and injustice in (say) job applications and job promotion.

2 The institution of strong, appropriately targeted, anti-crime campaigns, where they involve a darker-skinned person, exploited by a lighter-skinned person. Matthies suggests public awareness campaigns utilising everything from bill-boards, TV, radio, drama, while at the same time developing media which does not glorify such status arrangements. This would include newer media such as video gaming.

3 Education. The education of parents in child-rearing is essential if progress is to be made. This includes an understanding of the relevant laws. Similar training should also be available to professionals involved in child-care, including medical practitioners, health professionals, social workers, teachers, and police.

Church leaders should be included, as mindsets are directly involved with the kind of positive changes that every Christian minister should be seeking to implement, such as a Christian maturity that is open to development, fellowship across social and racial divides, taking personal responsibility, and being forgiving.

4 Service provision should include early screening programmes to detect pathologies before they get entrenched, especially in pre-adolescents. Victims of colour-coding related antisocial behaviours need counselling and support by trained health and social workers. Peer-based mentoring could be set up in schools, churches, and community organisations. This is particularly the case where colour-coding has or is resulting in abuse of any kind, including abuse dressed up as 'family discipline' or 'work discipline'.

---

114   *Cf.* Matthies *et al.,* 'Issues of Violence in the Caribbean', in Hickling *et al.,* *Perspectives in Caribbean Psychology.*

5   *Changing the structure of society.* In many ways, this is the *sine qua non*, the essential condition, without which one could be treating symptoms rather than causes. Strengthening protective social structures is more effective than focussing on risk reduction. ***Inequality in Family, Church, School***. Dealing with issues in each of these contexts is precisely what the colour code implies—inequality. Education of children must be at the heart of social changes. Small class sizes, more financial assistance, making a greater emphasis on life-skills and job skills, banning corporal punishment, and using non-violent methods of discipline are all required.

Is There Another Answer?

These five steps are all practical and possible, given enough people who are not only committed to make them work, but who are motivated by a faith which has touched them deeply enough to give them a colour-blind vision of human beings.

This all springs from understanding how God sees the world, and what God has done in the Person of his Son, Jesus Christ. The presentation of God in the Bible shows that God cares when things go wrong. God grieves when people are hurt and abused. God's answer was to reveal Himself as a convicted criminal, shamed, abused, and illegally killed – yes, judicially murdered by the decision of Pilate, the Roman Governor of Jerusalem, whose question, *"What is truth?"* (John 18:38) whether spoken with a serious intent, or mere cynicism, has great significance. ***The crucial factor is a totally committed motivation, which over-rides all other priorities.***[115]

What, indeed, is 'truth'? All the books in the world, or the world's biggest SIM card, might not have space to answer such a question.

Paradoxically, Jesus spoke of God as his Father, saying *"Anyone who has seen Me, has seen the Father"* (John 14:9). What! God nailed to a tree? Yes, indeed! One who understands from the inside the experience of the lashed, abused, and lynched – this reveals the love of God the Father, and his Son, for the two are one.

The teaching of Jesus turned upside down acceptable values of justice, an eye for an eye, a tooth for a tooth. He said, *"Love your enemies",* and *"Blessed are the peacemakers, for they will be called*

---

115   Cf. William Hasker (above) and Romans 7.13-25

children of God" (Matthew 5:44 and 5:9) – children? These are those who share in the characteristics of their parent, the life of the Father!

From the beginning of time God wanted to reveal himself through the prophets of Israel and finally through the life, death, and resurrection of Jesus. By allowing human beings to murder him cruelly God demonstrated his love in the most incredible way. Almost his last words were *"Father, forgive them, for they know not what they do"* (Luke 23:34). Does this obviate all that has been written in this chapter, perhaps in this book? No, it does not!

Out of the mouth of Jesus, portrayed as a lamb, sacrificed, a two-edged sword was issued – the word of Truth. Truth can be presented in many ways. Through the life of Jesus, God demonstrated truth. He said, *"I am the way, and the truth, and the life"* (John 14:6).

Truth implies the values of forgiveness, healing, reconciliation. As the Apostle Paul said, *"God was in Christ, reconciling the world to Himself"* (2 Corinthians 5:19). He chose to do this through his life and death – speaking the truth at the cost of torture and death. God has shown, in the suffering and death of Jesus, what it is to *truly* reveal Himself.

So? Whether we believe in Critical Race Theory (CRT), or the work of the Equality Trust, or Martin Luther King or variants of all these, we need to endeavour always to speak the truth: to question invested power structures (on the outside) and attitudes of personal investment (on the inside); whether driven by anger, shame, or despair. For there is an answer to even the most complex problems of humanity, and it lies in the God of all Truth – in taking up our cross and following him who showed that there were no limits in his love beyond which he was prepared to go!

In so doing he broke down the dividing wall of hostility between nations, races, classes, and individuals. It is a journey with many pitfalls and battles, but it is the way to healing for nations and for each one of us.

Chapter 15
A CASE STUDY
HARRIET MAYNARD – MULATIN WENDJE? KASTIEZEN?[116]

In this chapter Nigel Pocock presents a fascinating case study, then uses it to demonstrate and discuss the internal conflicts that probably face any mixed-race child in a white dominated society. It offers some penetrating insights into the stresses and strains of the 'two-world experience' that shapes the lives of millions of people of colour living in white dominated societies. Inevitably, it poses more questions than it answers, but the whole purpose of this book is to expose issues that are hidden on the surface, and to encourage thought-provoking consideration of the changing cultures in our 21st-century world.

As a mulatto my grandfather was never fully accepted by black or white. One day I hope to honour him and raise the head of my great-grandmother, his mother for their lives were also hard and unbearable. My great-grandmother lived in poverty and died shortly after child-birth, the child after my grandfather.

She left behind seven children. The eldest girl was white enough to 'pass' for white and did so. We do not know of her children. If we speak of the effect of race, I do not have to look at the systemic, just at my mother's family. The lighter-skinned ones have a separate existence from us darker-skinned ones. We share similar genetic material but are lost to each other.

—Tracy, Barbados

Mixed-Race Artist

On 27th July 1906, a mixed-race artist, Harriet Maynard, died. She had been ill with ovarian cancer, and was very likely in great pain, there being no pain relief other than morphine. Harriet was

---

116   Dutch, 'mulatto young woman'.

56 years old. Her tombstone, in St Stephen's Churchyard, Launceston, Cornwall, stands forlorn against a wall, away from most of the main burial ground. It contains an inscription, in lead: 'pray for the repose of the soul of Harriet Maynard'. About four hundred yards away, in the adjacent Roman Catholic churchyard (not in existence while Harriet was alive) lies the body of Harriett's probable mentor, Canon Charles Langdon, who passed away seven years after Harriet, aged 62 years. On the gravestones of both are exactly the same words, but with one crucial difference. For Canon Langdon, there is no request for 'repose'. This extremely unusual word has, surely, to be deliberate. Harriet knew no peace. But why? This is what we hope to explore in this chapter and apply to the topic of this book: the colour code.

While we have very little to go on regarding Harriet, other than bare facts, there are extremely strong probabilities. These are both social and psychological. On the premise that 'the body keeps the score',[117] we will first look at these facts, and ask ourselves how these facts translate into Harriet's traumatic life experience, and their relevance for today.

---

117 I am indebted to Prof. Bessel van der Kolk for this expression, which implies that negative trauma to the brain profoundly impacts the body, and vice-versa. Cf. Bessel van der Kolk, *The Body Keeps the Score*, Penguin, London 2014..

Birth

On the 30th August 1849, at 6.30 in the morning, baby Harriet makes her first appearance in the world. The room must have been well known to her mother, very likely her regular home, for her short-lived brother, who survived for ten months, William, had been born in the same room in the previous year. This building was known as 18, Saraakastraat, Section E, Paramaribo, Surinam. Harriet's father was 55 year old William Maynard, the son of an English merchant navy captain, now a very prosperous cotton planter, and an Amsterdam bank representative. William was in a 'Surinam marriage' to Harriet's mother Magdalena Martha Mijnhard, a 25 year old slave who was very likely manumitted just before baby William's birth in 1848. This practice meant that the hereditary chain of slavery could be broken.

Magdalena was a *mulatin wendje*, meaning that Harriet was probably seen as *kastiezen*. William had already known liaisons with other women, two black Africans, Catherina Carolina (the mother of his *mulatin* son, Arnold, born in 1821, when William was 27 who himself became a planter), and Nelly (the latter being known as 'van Maynard'). William then entered into a legal marriage with a Scot, Helen Paton, who died shortly afterwards, perhaps in childbirth. It was after Helen's death that William 'married' Magdalena. As we will see, this was to cause problems for William later. In all of this, slavery was still legal in Surinam (Dutch Guyana), until 1863, only to be finally abolished ten years later, after a period of 'apprenticeship'.

Type of Caste System

As elsewhere, it is unsurprising that this extremely violent culture of slavery, exploitation and abuse of women led to a kind of caste system organised around skin colour. William and Magdalena would have known very well what the lay of the land was for mixed race women, and have been fearful for Harriet if they had cared for her in any kind of way. For *mulatin* women were the 'favoured' group for sexual exploitation.

Moravians

The Moravian church was one of the most influential churches in Surinam, and Magdalena was a member of its local congregation in the capital, Paramaribo. By this time, the

Moravians were in an ambiguous position. Having started by being against slavery (without active opposition) they gradually accommodated themselves to the extent that they became slave-owners themselves. Thus the Moravians, fearful of offending the secular authorities, came to compromise themselves to the extent of cooperating with slavery.

One of the biggest cotton traders in Surinam was the Moravian-run and slave-owning Kersten & Company. William would have known this company well, perhaps even making Magdalena's acquaintance through them. Whatever the case, William decided to send Harriet to England, in order to be educated by the Moravians. Harriet was by now about 5 years old.

In about 1854, Harriet was placed, involuntarily, into a vessel in Paramaribo, very probably with the Moravian Minister, the Revd. Charles Lewis Schwartz, and his Dutch wife, Cornelia. Little Harriet would never see her mother again.

Arrival in England

Sometime in 1855, after her long sea journey of around 5,000 miles, lasting several weeks, little Harriet arrived in England. She travelled, possibly from London (where her father had business contacts) to Ockbrook in Derbyshire. Everything Harriet saw was new to her: cold, wet, and gloomy. There were amazing technological marvels, such as rail travel and iron bridges, huge smoke-belching chimneys from hundreds of factories, processing the cotton exported from Surinam by her father. Arriving in Ockbrook, Harriet met the Moravians, a community she already knew from her time in Paramaribo.

In Ockbrook, they had an established community, with a school. For years, the Moravians had built on their reputation for education, community, and mission, with remarkable success. Here she would learn more about their mission, and be educated in topics that, the Moravians hoped, would further this mission, such as geography, languages, medicine, and the Bible, but also the basics of mathematics, art, and music. At a time when education for girls was a low priority, and boys learned little else than the classics, this was a progressive curriculum. Indeed, it might even be that Moravian women were over-educated in respect of the opportunities open to them.

Marriage

During his time in Ockbrook, William Maynard formed an attachment to a Moravian worker, Rachel Spence, a single woman in her forties. The Moravian community were extremely suspicious of this liaison. Not only were there doubts about William's spiritual credentials, but what about his supposed 'marriage' to Magdalena? What about the little mixed-race girl who came to Ockbrook with him? Clearly William managed to persuade the Moravian elders of his credentials, as the couple were married with Moravian approval, in September 1855. William was now 61 years old, but, financially, a very good 'catch' for Rachel, who may well have thought that marriage was not a part of God's will for her until now.

Teenager

After another five years, Harriet, now 11 years old, was transferred to the much smaller Moravian settlement in East Tytherton, Wiltshire. Was this because it was nearer to London, where her father would have conducted much of his business? This state of affairs was not to last, for within three years, William Maynard was dead, aged 67 years. Harriet, by then was 14 years old, and at a very impressionable time in her life. With a mother whom she never saw, and a father who was rarely there for her (if at all), Harriet now had no parents of any kind.

Traditionally the Moravians had regarded their community as being as good as, and possibly better than, biological parents (some will observe that the *Communist Manifesto* says much the same thing!). What was significant for Harriet was her father's will. Intriguingly, William left almost nothing to his wife, and almost everything to Harriet. This might not be from a perverse mindset however, but from concern, not just for Harriet, but for a wife who may have been unwell. In the event, Harriet was left the modern equivalent of £250,000. By the time of her own death, Harriet had four properties which she was letting out, and thousands of pounds in Canadian stocks and shares, all of which might have had their origins in her father's shrewd investments. Harriet was now a 'gentlewoman', a woman of 'independent means'. And of mixed race.

Stepmother Carer

It is not clear what happened next, but from 1871 (when Harriet was 22) she was living with her 64 year-old step-mother in London, perhaps as her carer. Harriet would do this, until just before her death aged 72. Harriet was now 30 years of age. In the meantime, Harriet enrolled at the prestigious Female (later 'Royal Female') School of Art,[118] where she gained her Art Masters' Certificate, at the highest (third level), in 1877, at the age of 28. She was now recognized by the Government as qualified to teach art, if she so wished. Harriet nonetheless carried on studying at the school. She evidently enjoyed being there, perhaps she **felt safe, together with the female company.**

Cousins

Harriet's extensive cousins included at least three artists. One, Ernest Spence (1863-1944), was an RA. Ernest's wife, Amabel du Cane was also at the Female School of Art. It may be through them, as well as the known Moravian emphasis on crafts, that she was encouraged to pursue an artistic career. At least until 1881 Harriet was in touch with her Spence adoptive cousins, staying with and visiting them. In 1882 a painting by Harriet Maynard is recorded in a major exhibition in Bournemouth Town Hall, *Chrysanthemums*, and another in 1895 at a Society of Women Artists' exhibition, when Harriet was 46.

Penzance

By 1906, Harriet had moved to Penzance, and then to Launceston, where she died. Just four years before, her mother, 78 year old Magdalena, died in Surinam, and left her house to Harriet. In Tokenhouse Yard, London EC, Harriet's last worldly possessions were auctioned to the highest bidder. On a hill just outside Launceston, Harriet now lies in a lonely spot, waiting to tell her story, and for us to learn from it.

Psychosomatic Analysis

This is the essential outline of Harriet's history, as far as we know. But what of a psychosomatic or psychophysiological history, in which the impacts of Harriet's life events caused ripples that never end, throughout her life?

---

118   Now part of St. Martin's College of Art, itself part of the University of London.

William Maynard

There is no evidence that William Maynard is cynically using Magdalena (or his earlier liaison, Catherina) as a means of merely siring or breeding 'stock' for profit. Quite the opposite. William is 55 years old by the time of Harriet's birth, already established and wealthy. His son, Arnold, by Catherina, is by now 28 years old, himself manager of a coffee plantation, at Wederzorg—very likely manumitted by William, as presumably such a position of authority would not be possible to a slave? It may be that Catherina died young, for William had another relationship, with Nelly, who adopted (or was given) William's name, van Maynard, but had no children with him, as far as is known. Perhaps she, too died?

Manumission

So far, so good—at least, relatively speaking. That is, relative to the violent slave culture outside. Until she is five years old, Harriet presumably had Magdalena's attention, and very likely her father's too. This is a crucial time for a very small child. Then! Slavery! William manumitted (legally set free) Magdalena, probably with a view to securing her child's freedom. William did not want his children to be born as slaves! But this did not end the coercive pressure of the culture of slavery, race, or shades of colour. Fearing for Harriet, William arranged for her to travel to England, aged five years. Will this facilitate an escape from this evil culture? In part, perhaps, yes; in another, no.

Magdalena Martha Mijnhard is already a Moravian, and no doubt played a part in helping lay the plans, as William was not a Moravian, although he probably knew them well. The Moravians had a long tradition of believing that the Settlement and its schooling could socialise even the smallest children better than their biological parents. (Founder Count Zinzendorf, 1700-1760, unrealistically believed that even 1½ year olds could be educated into Moravian doctrine and practice. He was very disappointed to find that they could not!)[119] By Harriet's time, such an attitude would have ameliorated, as non-Moravian children were now accepted into Moravian Schools.

---

119 Gillian Lindt Gollin, *Moravians in Two Worlds*, London & New York, Columbia University Press, 1967..

Traumatic Period

Nonetheless, this period in Harriet's life was almost certainly extremely traumatic for a five-year old – torn away from both parents (although her father may have travelled to England and Ockbrook with her), and especially her mother, for her supposed 'good'. This was probably anything but 'good'. Recent research on children evacuated in WWII shows that, although well-intentioned, the children who remained with their parents, even as bombs rained down, were less traumatised than the 'safer' evacuees.[120] Everything depends on the understanding of the sense of 'safety' – and loving parents provide this best of all. There is no substitute for a triangle of love, which encompasses a mother-father-child. Did slavery and then colonialism, with colour codes, even in the 'home country' perpetuate a fragmented and dysfunctional family? It did indeed!

Traumatised

Was Harriet thereby traumatised by her childhood experience, a 'well-intentioned path to harm'? What might the effects, indeed probable effects, of broken attachment, have been upon five years old Harriet? This is deeply relevant, as this is an important factor throughout the broken families of the Caribbean, even today.

This is where we return to Harriet's need for 'repose'. Here was a person deeply in need of personal peace, and her biography gives us every reason to suppose that Harriet's problems, physical, spiritual, sociological, and psychological (all impacting each other) have their origins in the culture of slavery. Out of this culture arose 'miscegenation' – racial mixing. Out of racial mixing, a hierarchy of 'shades' – 'shadism', from lowest 'blackest', to highest 'whitest'. Harriet was in-between. Neither black nor white, she was pulled both ways. The new, adoptive, family culture would have pulled her towards 'white'. Her personal childhood history, the connection to her mother, towards 'black'. Her cultural and racial background would have set up tensions that would never leave her – starting with her parenting – or lack thereof.

Mother's Influence

There is much to suggest that Harriet's early years were probably in close proximity to her mother, but how good was this? It is all

---

120 Van der Kolk, *The Body Keeps the Score*, 210.

too likely that Magdalena was the product of an abusive childhood herself, a *mulatin wendje*—a person who might have been damaged to the extent that she was unable to look after Harriet with closeness and empathy. If this were the case, then Harriet's very first days were deprived, right from the start. However, on the premise that 'the body keeps the score', Magdalena's death at 78, suggests that her psychosocial health was good, by the standards of the time, perhaps helped by the personal and corporate spiritual support of the Moravian community.

Father's Influence

Harriet's father, William, then had to decide on Harriet's future. This was a male-dominated culture, and William was a top businessman, meaning that he very likely had a fairly hard-headed personality. Cultures select for 'success'. In John Gabriel Stedman's famous account of a somewhat parallel situation, the author leaves his much-loved Surinamese slave mistress in Surinam when he has to return to Britain – but only because he realised that Joanna could not bear to be parted from the social world that she knew.[121] Perhaps William Maynard's situation was somewhat similar? On the assumption that it was, this may have been the choice between a 'rock and a hard place' – both being much less than ideal, and both evil – with departure for England being decided on as the lesser of the two.

Silent Grief

Being torn away from her mother, Harriet was very likely traumatised. Her tears and crying for many days, perhaps months, eventually subsiding, replaced by silent grief – subsequently misinterpreted by relieved carers, who think she is now 'over it'.[122] Not so. Traumatic memories last for life, sometimes not spoken, because the area of the brain to do with verbalising (Brocca's area)[123] is shut down. Only the limbic system and the amygdala, one of the earliest and most primitive parts of the brain, keep reacting, with violent mood swings – non-verbalizable, autonomic, not understood, or misunderstood, by both victim and carers.

---

121   J.G. Stedman, *Narrative of an Expedition Against the Revolted Negroes of Surinam*, University of Massachusetts, c. 1790, reprinted 1971.

122   Sandra Bloom

123   Van der Kolk, *The Body Keeps the Score,* 43-44.

Moravian Influence

True, some recovery is possible, in a warm and supportive and safe environment. But there is no substitute for a mother who cares, however good the Moravian community might have been. Generally speaking, in providing a loving bond, mother does indeed know best.

Marriage counsellor Walter Trobisch comments that (controversially for some, motivated by individualism?) that it is 'more important for the child to know that its parents love each other, than to know that it is loved'. If this is true, then it is likely to be related to the need to provide a sense of safety, the key insight of Polyvagal Theory.[124] This theory has been developed around what Darwin knew as the 'pneumogastric nerve' – the tenth cranial nerve, or vagus ('wandering') nerve. This nerve connects all the major organs of the body, heart, lungs, stomach, colon, but also the head, head and neck muscles, with the brain, all being part of the autonomic nervous system.

Environment

The importance of this insight is that treating the body is just as important as treating the brain, as much of what impacts the brain is autonomic, derived from tensions in the viscera – heart, stomach – as chronic tension causes heart rate to rise (or, conversely, to shut down, as in dissociation), the stomach to overreact, and so on.

Continuous impact by a threatening environment eventually creates a new default setting for the brain-body-autonomic system, leading to diseases that will destroy the person or at the least, to shorten life expectancy and the person's quality of life. Everything from heart failure to cancer can be a part of this destructive pathology, epigenetics (inhibited gene expression)[125] to organ inflammation (related to depression and other illnesses),[126] including Harriet's own premature death from ovarian cancer, a disease notably correlated to single women with no children.[127] Overarching all is slavery, abuse of women, miscegenation, colour codes and racial castes.

What then might Harriet's psychosomatic biography have been, in the face of such small clues and probabilities?

---

124   Associated with Steven Porges.

125   Nessa Carey, *The Epigenetics Revolution*, Icon, London 2012.

126   Edward Bullmore, *The Inflamed Mind*, London, Short Books, London 2018.

127   *Family Medical Encyclopaedia*, ed. Michael Peters, Dorling Kindersley, 4th edn., London 2004.

Culture of Slavery

Born into a culture of slavery, she would have experienced its prejudice, separated from both parents, she would have experienced the profound trauma of this loss and grief. At the very end of her life, she leaves a Will in which she leaves nothing to her adoptive cousinhood, and, apart from a legal obligation to her solicitor, and a donation to a Roman Catholic charity, all her worldly possessions are left to four close female friends, all of whom are cultured and educated. Throughout her life, Harriet lives with women, and trains at the Royal Female School of Art. At the very last, her loss of peace is noted, and prayer requested. Is this something that became a default setting, and pursued her throughout her life?

Christian Faith

There is no mention of her Moravian inheritance, and she has not abandoned her Christian faith, but why a movement towards Roman Catholicism? Perhaps a close friendship with the celibate Canon Langdon, with whom she felt safe? For, indeed, it seems that it was a lifelong battle to find safety, physical, social, spiritual, and psychological, that drove Harriet in her education, friendships, and spiritual choices, and set the barriers of safety around her. Homeless, she never lived (as far as we know) in any property that she herself owned (unless her time with her step-mother was in Harriet's home, and not Rachel's). Homelessness, spiritual and physical – was what characterised Harriet – even her £250,000 (modern values) inheritance might have alienated her cousinhood, creating familial jealousy and envy?

Colour Coding

Drawing on traumatology and Polyvagal Theory, a number of possibilities arise, but first we need to touch base with the theme of this book. To what extent did 'race' and 'colour coding' enter into Harriet's self-perception? We have no known photograph of Harriet, unless the very vague and minute one (below) is of her in front of the Moravian church building. If we are correct in our interpretation, then Harriet looks quite dark, and has a definite African look to her hair. But the image is so far from clear, this can be no more than surmise. If true, then Harriet could not have been capable of 'passing' as white.

Is it possible the young girl or woman (detail enlarged below) could be Harriet Maynard? The photo could have been taken in the 1860s, when Harriet (aged 11-12 +) was at the school.

In trauma, as mentioned already, the brain area to do with speech, Brocca's area, can shut down, and the articulation of verbal memories are lost. Harriet's default setting may have become one of over-reactivity and hypervigilance. This could have been matched with a dislike of being touched. Sleep, digestion and more could have been affected. Harriet could have been left with lifelong poor health and difficulties in 'coping' – the bottom line for good mental health. Her emotionality could also have been affected positively, eliciting strong emotions towards those who were her friends, and who she trusted, and therefore felt safe with.

Conversely, trauma increases spontaneous outbursts of anger for seeming trivialities,[128] which Harriet might not herself have understood, and also regretted. Trauma increases the risk of misinterpreting danger signals,[129] so Harriet might not have been

---

128 Van der Kolk, *The Body Keeps the Score*, 42, 53, 56-7.
129 *Ibid.*, 61-2.

easy to get on with, given her unpredictable changes and outbursts. According to polyvagal theory there are two ways of coping with trauma, and of threats to one's sense of safety. One is rooted in fight or flight, marked by raised heart-rate, adrenaline and cortisol.

Freezing

The other is marked by the complete reverse, the shut-down of all systems – a dissociated state of near unconsciousness.[130] This is a form of freezing and is a way of blocking out the threat to one's personal safety, but also, sadly, the good as well. Harriet might therefore have found unfamiliar groups difficult to cope with, unless she felt completely safe in them, as she must have done in the Royal Female School. She might well have retreated into a 'safe' state of numbness in order to cope with the threat.[131] The Female School was probably safe and predictable, and this facilitated coping.

Could this be why Harriet stayed on at the Royal Female School for at least two more years after she qualified? Was Harriet's tendency never to live in any property she owned (she had at least four), an expression of her sense of her loss of safety and home'? One of the saddest features of becoming dissociated, is, as Bessel van der Kolk notes, lies in any sense of being alive.[132] It is one step away from being dead when the heart stops altogether.

Institutional Influence

Throughout all of her life, Harriet's traumatic memories would have stayed with her – leaving her mother and home, arriving in England, being placed in a highly regimented institution.[133] These would have compounded a sense of worthlessness, and a sense of being to blame, for being rejected. Traumatic childhoods are correlated (as noted) to obesity and cancer.[134] Uptight and anxious women have been found to lack social support – but change if they join a stable social group, as the Female School clearly was. Traumatised children are clingy and needy, lacking in trust, having

---

130 *Ibid.,* 66.

131 *Ibid.,* 88.

132 Van der Kolk, *The Body Keeps the Score,* 91-2.

133 *Ibid.,* 175.

134 *Ibid.,* 147.

few friends.[135] White inside, black outside, Harriet's sense of acceptance was disorganised and confused. With a 'dual identity' in which, on the one hand, Harriet sought predictability with her few female friends, and on the other, with a 'ruinous ever-present past', Harriet's life was, seemingly, mapped out before her.

Shame

A tale for the foolish, and a parable for the wise? Which is Harriet's psychosomatic biography to be? Shame is one of the key factors that will determine responses: Shame of the failure to prevent slavery, by people of African origin; Shame of being the perpetrators, by the other, the Europeans. Shame drives denial, and denial drives the failure to find answers.

So, the 'answers' are based on lies and falsehoods. Shame drives 'shadism', and the Jamaican dance-hall culture of 'Michael Cake Soap Jackson', and the attempts to legitimise skin bleaching and 'browning'.[136]

The Answer

There is an answer, and it flies in the face of both the 'fight' and 'dissociation' responses developed by evolution. It is not popular, but is, as Jesus taught, 'the narrow way that leads to life'. It is, or can be, hard. It means wearing a yoke, but a yoke that Jesus said, paradoxically, is easy. In putting it on burdens become light! How could this be? Because in putting on humility and service, the desire for aggression, with its raised heart-rate, stress hormones, comfort-eating, back-biting, resentment against others, and much more, is abandoned for the love and service of others!

This indeed is the answer, and it applies as much to power-hungry church leaders as to the blackest of black-skinned labouring poor. The way is narrow, but like the way to Narnia, it is through a small door, like a child. Push the door open and enter in!

---

135 *Ibid.*, 158.

136 Donna P Hope, 'From Browning to Cake Soap: Popular debates on Skin Bleaching in the Jamaican Dancehall', *Journal of Pan African Studies*, Vol. 4, No. 4, 2011, 165-194.

Chapter 16
BREAKING BARRIERS

In this final chapter Clifford Hill exercises his role as editor by drawing together the threads of the different themes explored in this book. It does not attempt to present easy answers to the intractable social issues that are covered in this book. It does, however, offer a sociological perspective that provides the basis for strategies of social change. It also recognises the immense difficulties of changing the values of society, but it ends on a note of hope based upon the shared personal faith of the three authors of this book.

Colour Consciousness

In this book we have been tracing the origins of skin colour consciousness that forms a major factor in social differentiation and social status in mixed-race societies. We have traced the roots of this phenomenon to colonial slavery where the white plantocracy exerted total dominance over the African slaves in the Caribbean and the Americas. We have further noted that it was the lascivious sexual activities of the white rulers with powerless African women that created large numbers of mixed racial children. The children who were of very fair skin were not sent to work in the slave field gangs but were given privileged posts within the household.

It was this practice that began the whole process of social differentiation based upon skin colour. Inevitably such a system that offered privileges to those of the fairest skin had psychological effects upon the whole slave population. Fair skinned people had black servants waiting upon them and they thought of themselves as superior. The institutionalised injustice of this system of social differentiation and its effect upon the lives of millions of people is beyond description.

Institutionalised Injustice

We have also noted some of the institutionalised injustices that affect many nations today and give rise to incidents such as the murder of George Floyd in Minneapolis in 2020 that triggered violent demonstrations in many cities across the USA and in other parts of the world. It was these demonstrations that led to the spread of the Black Lives Matter campaign that we noted at the beginning of this book.

Alton Bell has written two chapters describing his experience as a black man living in a white dominated society, and the social scientist Nigel Pocock has looked at some of the psychosomatic problems associated with racial differences and the implications of the sad case-study of Harriet, the mixed-race girl who was neither black nor white. The major question underlying the presentation in this book is, what can be done to ameliorate the injustices that have been created in mixed race societies? Clearly, we cannot undo history; neither can we abolish social differentiation, even though the practice of discrimination in such sectors such as employment and education have been made illegal.

What we cannot do through legislation is to change the attitudes of people which are based upon their personal and social values. We can make changes in the structure of society so that the practice of discrimination in all public areas of social interaction are made illegal with the expectation that this will slowly change attitudes especially if the education of children goes in tandem with the legislation and children grow up in a discrimination-free environment.

Britain and America

The situation in the USA is very different from that of Britain. In America, the old civil war wounds between the Confederate and Union states can still be seen, and it is only one generation since segregation between black and white in the southern states has been made illegal. Attitudes, however, take a lot longer to change as can be seen in the police dealings with black people.

In Britain, slavery based on race has never been practised and people of colour were rarely seen anywhere in the UK prior to the Second World War. The sailing of the 'Empire Windrush' from Jamaica in 1948 began the inflow of black people into Britain, soon followed by Asians. So multiracial communities have only been known in Britain for little more than a single generation.

I personally grew up in London in the 1930s and throughout my boyhood I do not remember ever seeing a black person. After leaving university I began living and working in a mixed racial area in 1952 – only four years after the arrival of the first black worker migrants. I can therefore claim to have seen the massive changes that have taken place in my lifetime. But I recognise the problems of colour differentiation are far deeper and more intransigent than can be changed by legislation.

Making a Change

There are two levels at which change can take place: one is in practices of discrimination in the public arena, and the second is in the psychological effects upon individuals within the black communities where differences of colour and pigmentation affect behaviour and self-esteem at all levels in the colour code. But we need to explore the possibilities of fundamental changes that can be effected in society.

We have already noted that legislation can affect behaviour and slowly change attitudes in the public arena. But changing attitudes of white people towards the black communities and attitudes within the black communities themselves, is a much deeper issue which is unresponsive to legislation. Attitudes are largely based upon personal and social values, and this provides the point of intervention at which changes in attitudes can take place. What is needed therefore, is a process of social change that affects the values of society. We will therefore take a brief look at the processes of social change.

Concepts of Social Change

Among the numerous theories of social change, the outstanding systems of thought have not changed much in the past 40 or 50 years. Modern sociologists still turn to the three outstanding systems of Marx, Malinowski and Parsons as providing the major framework for studying social change. Of course, there are plenty of variants and applications designed to meet the changes in society that have taken place since the middle of the 20th century. But the work of the three giants of sociological theory has not been surpassed. So, in this concluding chapter of the book we want to look to the future of race relations and attitudes of colour consciousness. We make the starting point a recognition of the basic theories of social change.

I summarised the three outstanding systems of thought in *Towards the Dawn* as being:

- The Theory of Economic Determinism initially expounded by Karl Marx.
- The Functionalist Theory that originated with Bronislaw Malinowski.
- The Social Action Theory of Talcott Parsons.[137]

Economic Determinism

Marx saw the main agent of social change as being located in the economic systems of society. He believed that the type of economy determined the culture, the values and even the belief system of society. He therefore believed that all changes in society began in the economy. His celebrated pronouncement was 'The mode of production of the material means of life determines in general the social, political and intellectual processes of life.'[138]

Functionalist Theory

The theory of functionalism developed by Malinowski was based upon the concept of need. The most basic needs of human beings are organic or biological – the need to get and to beget, the need for food, shelter, and the satisfaction of biological impulses. Malinowski believed that cultural change had to begin from the basic organic needs of human beings which he grouped under three headings: instrumental, recreational, and integrative. The **instrumental** needs were economic, educational, and political. The **integrative** needs were knowledge, science, and religion. The **recreative** imperatives were art, music, and games. The significance of Malinowski's theory was that he sees them as *imperatives* rather than options which individuals can choose or ignore.

---

137 Clifford Hill, *Towards the Dawn: What's going to happen to Britain?* William Collins and Sons, Fount Paperbacks, London 1980, 22.

138 Karl Marx, *Critique of Political Economy,* Lawrence and Wishart, London 1940, 13.

The theory of functionalism assumes that all social processes are causally determined, and human beings are driven by causally determined laws both in terms of social culture and from the physical environment.

Social Action Theory

The Social Action Theory, or 'Pattern Variables', developed by Talcott Parsons posited the concept of 'value theory' which assumes a set of common values contained within the cultural system which contribute towards the overall unity of all social systems. The dominant values are those held in common by most members of a given society. These values may change over a period of time primarily as a result of changing perceptions of ultimate reality, and these values legitimise the whole normative structure of the society.

Individuals, as well as social groups, are guided by the values of society which have become internalised in individuals through socialisation and incorporated into systems by the process of institutionalisation. The shared values of society, drawn from the cultural system, shape and control all social life. According to Parsons: 'A system of value orientation held in common by the members of a social system can serve as the main point of reference for analysing structure and process in the social system itself.'[139] Thus, in order to effect basic changes in the structures of a society, we have to change the values of that society.

Changing Values

This is a conclusion of immense significance if we are to consider strategies of social change that could affect the whole system of colour coding that influences the lives of millions of black and brown people. Parsons believes that there is a realm of 'ultimate reality' which gives meaning and objectivity to values. Those who adhere to a monotheistic religion such as Judeo-Christianity and Islam would readily agree to such a concept of ultimate reality which not only gives 'meaning and objectivity' to social values but is the source of those values.

---

139 Talcott Parsons, *Structure and Process in Modern Societies*, Glencoe Free Press, Glencoe, Illinois 1959, 172.

This is where a strategy of social change that would have widespread public support could begin – with an examination of the values of society. This could be undertaken in the context of values derived from religious tradition such as the Judaeo-Christian belief that all human beings are created by God and have equal value in his sight. Other values such as justice, truth, integrity, love, and faithfulness, should also be considered as coming from the realm of ultimate reality.

The Teaching of Jesus

Changing the values of society was a major part of the teaching of Jesus. In fact, he turned upside down many of the values that were current in society at his time. At the Last Supper, which Jesus ate with his disciples, he actually took a basin of water and a towel, and he knelt and washed the feet of each of his disciples. Thus, in a very practical way he turned upside down the values of the world wherein the humblest slave in the household was usually employed to wash the feet of visitors.

It was unheard-of for a Master to wash the feet of his servants, or of any of those in lower social ranks. But Jesus consistently taught that those who were last should come first, and first come last. The whole of his life and ministry were a demonstration of servant leadership. This is a concept unknown to the world where power is exercised to control the lives of others. In servant leadership power is exercised to enable others to develop their gifts and find fulfilment in working alongside others to achieve the common good. Jesus specifically taught the value of meekness and humility, and anonymity in doing good deeds. He reversed the popular values of justice based upon 'Eye for eye, and tooth for tooth'. He said, *"You have heard that it was said, 'love your neighbour and hate your enemy'. But I tell you: Love your enemies and pray for those who persecute you"* (Matt 5:43). This was a complete reversal of the values of the world that are based upon dictatorship and the self-centred adulation of individuals.

This teaching of Jesus has been in the public domain for the past 2000 years, but it has never been practised on any wide scale in any nation. It has not been tried and found wanting and therefore discarded. Quite the reverse; it has been found too hard and not practised. In fact, far from the values of peace and serving one another being adopted in any culture, human beings have adulated violence and the acquisition of power and wealth. The result has been a massive increase in inequality and injustice for multitudes of human beings while a very small number enjoy overwhelming power and wealth.

The Bible teaches us that the two things that God hates most are injustice and the shedding of innocent blood. It also teaches equality; that God has no favourites, that all people of all races, male and female, are of equal value in the eyes of God.

The colour code system of social differentiation comes within the realm of injustice and the promotion of inequality, which is totally at variance with the teaching of Jesus. If we are to see any substantial change in the value system being followed by the nations, it has to start with a recognition of the need to re-evaluate the values that are being practised in the contemporary world. If there is a high degree of satisfaction among human beings in any period of time, there will be no change in society. It is only when dissatisfaction with the *status quo* occurs that people began to question the policies being followed that have produced the present situation.

This is the good news that we can take from the pandemic that hit the world in 2020 – it created an enormous level of disturbance in the routine of life in the Western nations where people were enjoying mass consumption of the proceeds of wealth while two thirds of the world's population were going hungry every day. The pandemic added to the rising level of dissatisfaction and unrest in most nations that was already becoming a characteristic of the 21st century.

A new factor in the social unrest to be seen in the Western nations is the growing concern over climate change and the desire to see policies that will protect nature from the vast levels of pollution that are damaging the natural environment. Alongside these issues that have caused people to reflect upon the policies being followed by political leaders the 'Black Lives Matter Movement' with its call for social justice for black people has made people reflect upon injustices of the past such as colonial slavery. Those who are concerned about the great injustices of the past, the roots of which have been buried in history for a long time, should actually be rejoicing to see these waves of social unrest and discontent that are disturbing the social equilibrium in many nations.

There has to be a recognition that something is wrong and there is a need for change before forces of change are set in motion. Of course, there is a danger of violent revolutionary forces being released into a nation that may produce an even more repressive regime than that which they overthrow. In that context, the end result becomes worse than the original.

The Hope of the World

If, however, the creative forces of social change are based upon a trustworthy value system, such as one that is based upon the teaching of Jesus, the resultant peace and prosperity could set a model for the whole of humanity. The beginning of change for society is the same for individual lives. It is the recognition that something is wrong. It is at that point that people develop a hunger for the truth as the reverse of fake news, deception, and oppression.

The unpalatable truth is that gentleness, kindness, generosity, unselfish service of others are characteristics that do not come naturally to human beings. We all have a propensity towards self-preservation, self-service, and self-interest. Something actually has to happen in our human nature to overcome these instinctive drives. This is where the Christian faith has unique value in its ability to change lives by changing the value system behind our instinctive drives. The plain truth is that it is changed people who bring about changes of policy in the nations. A change in the value system will only be effected by changed people. That is the unpalatable truth that we have to face.

Many Christians do not know how to share their Christian faith with others. But every Christian should have a story to tell of what Jesus has done in their own life. This is a day of unique opportunity in the turbulent days created by the Covid 19 pandemic that has affected every nation in the world and people of all social classes, rich and poor, young, and old, irrespective of nationality, race, or religion.

But these days when the pillars of society are being shaken were prophesied some 2500 years ago by a Hebrew prophet called Haggai and recorded in the Bible. The prophecy said, "This is what the Lord

Almighty says, *'In a little while I will once more shake the heavens and the earth, the sea and the dry land. I will shake all nations"* (Haggai 2:6-7).

This was picked up by the writer of the Book of Hebrews in the Christian New Testament who said that the great shaking of the nations would herald the beginning of a new age for humanity. People would reject the old ways that lead to death and destruction and look for a new way that leads to the new life that comes from Jesus.

The social unrest that we see around us today is creating a longing for truth in an age of fake news and deception. This openness to the truth gives an opportunity for Christians to share their experience of the change in their own lives that a personal encounter with Jesus has done for them. It begins with a recognition of personal need that is rapidly followed by a deep sense of peace through the presence of Jesus, and the forgiveness of past wrongdoing or inadequacy.

This is the beginning of the deep and fundamental change that takes place in each individual life which brings a desire to meet up with others who have had a similar experience. So, communities of faith are formed that begin to change the values of the nation. This is the good news that Christians have to impart. It is the good news that sets people free from being slaves to the cultural systems of oppression that we have been examining in this book and this is the faith that unites the three authors of this book – black and white – enabling us to embrace each other as brothers, brothers in Christ. And this is why faith in Jesus is the hope of the world!

SELECT BIBLIOGRAPHY

Adams, Michael Vannoy, *The Multicultural Imagination: Race, Colour and the Unconscious*, Routledge, London 1996.

Arogundade, *Black Beauty: A History and Celebration*, Pavilion, London 1996.

Batson, C. Daniel, 'Patricia Schoenrade' in W. Larry Ventis, *Religion and the Individual*, Oxford University Press, Oxford 1993.

Baumeister, Roy, *Evil: Inside Human Violence and Cruelty*, Barnes & Noble, New York 1997.

Bell, Alton T, *Breaking The Chains of Mental Slavery*, A and M Publishing, London 2013.

Blaisdell, B. (eds.), *Selected Writings and Speeches of Marcus Garvey*, Dover Thrift, New York 2004.

Botton, Alain de, *Status Anxiety*, Penguin, London 2005.

Broom, L., 'The Social Differentiation of Jamaica', *American Sociological Review*; Vol. 19; No. 2, Apr. 1954.

Bullmore, Edward, *The Inflamed Mind*, Short Books, London 2018.

Bryan, M. & Sanchez M., *Afro-Descendants, Discrimination & Economic Exclusion in Latin America*; Macro Study by Minority Rights Group Intl., 2003.

Carey, Nessa, *The Epigenetics Revolution*, Icon, London 2012.

Carter, J. D., 'Maturity, Psychological and Biblical', in H. Newton Malony (ed.), *Wholeness and Holiness: Readings in the Psychology/Theology of Mental Health*, Baker, Michigan 1993.

Charles, C.A.D, 'Skin Bleaching, Self-Hate & Black Identity in Jamaica', *Journal of Black Studies*, Vol. 33; No. 6, 2003.

Christian, M, 'An African-Centred Approach to the Black British Experience: With Special Reference to Liverpool', *Journal of Black Studies*; Vol. 28 No. 3, Jan. 1998.

Clarke, Edith, *My Mother Who Fathered Me*, University of the West Indies Press, Jamaica 1957.

Drake, St Clair, and Clayton, Horace R., *Black Metropolis*, University of Chicago Press, Chicago 1945.

Dweck , Carol, *Mindset*, Robinson, London 2012.

Fanon, F, *Black Skin, White Masks,* Pluto Press, London 1986.

Gabriel, Deborah, *Layers of Blackness: Colourism in the African Diaspora*, Imani Press Limited, London 2007.

Gollin, Gillian Lindt, *Moravians in Two Worlds*, Columbia University Press, London & New York 1967.

Hall, R, 'The Bleaching Syndrome: African Americans' Response to Cultural Domination Vis-à-vis Skin Colour', *Journal of Black Studies*, Vol. 26 No .2, Nov. 2007.

Hasker, William, *The Triumph of God over Evil*, IVP, Downers Grove, IL 2008.

Headley, B.D, 'Toward a Cyclical Theory of Race Relations in Jamaica', *Journal of Black Studies*, Vol. 15; No. 2; Dec. 1984.

Henriques, Fernando, *Family and Colour in Jamaica*, McGibbon and Kee, London 1968.

Hickling, Frederick W., 'Psychopathology of the Jamaican People', in Hickling et al., *Perspectives in Caribbean Psychology*, Jessica Kingsley, London 2008.

Higman, B.W., *Slave Population and Economy in Jamaica 1807-1834*, University of the West Indies Press, 1995.

Hill, Clifford, *Black and White in Harmony*, Hodder and Stoughton, London 1958.

Hill, Clifford, *West Indian Migrants and the London Churches*, Institute of Race Relations, Oxford University Press, Oxford 1963.

Hill, Clifford, *How Colour Prejudiced is Britain?* Victor Gollancz Limited, London 1965.

Hill, Clifford, *Immigration and Integration: A Study of the Settlement of Coloured Minorities in Britain,* Pergamon Press Ltd, Oxford 1970.

Hill, Clifford, 'Immigrant Sect Development in Britain: a Case of Status Deprivation?' in *Social Compass* XVIII, 1971/2.

Hill, Clifford, *Black Churches*, Community and Race Relations Unit, British Council of Churches, London, 1971.

Hill, Clifford, *The Wilberforce Connection*, Monarch Books, Oxford, 2004.

Hooks, Bell, *Ain't I A Woman: Black Women and Feminism*, Pluto Press, London 1981.

Hope, Donna P., 'From Browning to Cake Soap: Popular debates on Skin Bleaching in the Jamaican Dancehall', *Journal of Pan African Studies*, Vol. 4, No. 4 2011, 165-194.

Hunter M., *Race, Gender & the Politics of Skin Tone*, Routledge, 2005.

Hunter, M, 'If You're Light You're Alright: Light Skin Colour as Social Capital for Women of Colour', *Gender and Society*; Vol. 16, No. 2, 2002.

Jordan, W.D, 'American Chiaroscuro: The Status and Definition of Mulattos in the British Colonies', *The William and Mary Quarterly*, 3rd series Vol. 19, No. 2, Apr. 1962.

Lewis, Matthew G., *The Negro in the Caribbean*, Negro Universities Press 1969.

Long, Edward, *History of Jamaica*, Cambridge University Press, Cambridge 2010.

McDonald, J.A., 'Potential Influence of Racism and Skin Tone on Early Personality Formation', *Psychoanalytic Review* 2006, Vol. 93, No. 1.

Matthew, C.S, 'Marcus Garvey Writes from Jamaica on the Mulatto Escape Hatch', *Journal of Negro History*; Vol. 59, No. 2, Apr. 1974.

Matthies, Brigitte K., Julie Meeks-Gardner, Avril Daley, Claudette Crawford-Brown, 'Issues of Violence in the Caribbean', in Hickling et al., Perspectives in Caribbean Psychology, Jessica Kingsley, London 2008.

Morgan, Kai and Keisha-Gaye N. O'Garo, 'Caribbean Identity Issues', in Frederick W. Hickling, Brigitte Matties, Kai Morgan, Roger C. Gibson (eds.), *Perspectives in Caribbean Psychology*, Jessica Kingsley, London 2012.

Myers, David G., in *Psychology,* Vol. 4 1995, Worth, New York.

Peck, M. Scott, *Further Along the Road Less Travelled*, Simon & Schuster, London 1993.

Persaud, Raj, *Staying Sane*, Metro, London 1997.

Peters, Michael (ed.), *Family Medical Encyclopaedia*, fourth edn, Dorling Kindersley, London 2004.

Pinker, Steven, *The Blank Slate*, Penguin, London 2002.

Pointer, Roy, *How Do Churches Grow?* MARC Europe, London 1984.

Riley, Matthew Patrick, 'From Make America Great Again to Make America Better: How US History Shapes Christianity and Politics', The Conversation, University College, London (20th November 2020).

Rokeach, Milton, *The Open and Closed Mind*, Basic Books, New York, 1960.

Schama, Simon, *Rough Crossings,* BBC Books, London 2005.

Sheehan, Laurie, *The Slave Boy, The Life of Olaudah Equiano,* Librario Publishing Ltd, Kinloss Moray 2002.

Stedman, J.G., *Narrative of an Expedition Against the Revolted Negroes of Surinam*, (reprint 1971), University of Massachusetts c. 1790 (reprinted 1971).

Taylor, Yuval, *I Was Born a Slave: An Anthology of Classic Slave Narratives*, 2 Vols., Edinburgh 1999. Canongate.

Thurman, W., *The Blacker the Berry*, Scribner, New York 1996.

Van der Kolk, *The Body Keeps the Score*, Penguin, London 2014.

Wallis, Jim, *Christ in Crisis: Reclaiming Jesus*, HarperCollins, London 2019.

Walvin, James, *Black Ivory: Slavery in the British Empire*, Blackwell Publishing, Oxford 2001.

Waters, H., *Racism on the Victorian Stage: Representation of Slavery & the Black Character*; Cambridge University Press, Cambridge 2007.

Wesley, C.H., 'The Emancipation of the Free Coloured Population in the British Empire', *Journal of Negro History*, Vol. 19, No. 2, Apr. 1934.

Whyte, Iain, *Scotland and the Abolition of Black Slavery, 1756-1838*, Edinburgh University Press, Edinburgh 2007.

Williams, C., *The Destruction of Black Civilization: Great Issues of a Race from 4500 B.C to 2000 A.D,* Third World Press, Chicago 1987.

Wilson, A., *The Falsification of the Afrikan Consciousness*; Afrikan World Info Systems, New York 1993.

Windsor, R., *From Babylon to Timbuktu: A History of the Ancient Black: Races Including the Black Hebrews*, 20th edn, Windsor's Golden Series, Atlanta 2003.

INDEX

A

Acquired Anti-Own Race Syndrome 141–142, 149–151, 170
Africans. *See* immigration
  and West Indians 5, 61–63, 77–78, 90–92

B

black churches 51–52, 62. *see under* London
Black Lives Matter viii, x, 3, 16, 116–117, 131–132, 139, 146, 178
British laws 7–8, 17, 26, 30, 43, 88, 93

C

Cameron, David 14
Caribbean
  colour consciousness ix, 30–39, 133–143, 157–171
  education in 32, 125, 140
  family life 64–82
  immigrant generations 40, 53–63
  slavery in vii, 90–98, 99–103, 159–160
  statistics xi
change 10–13, 152–155, 172–180, 177. *See also* social change
  a Christian perspective 153–156, 171, 177–180
  and motivation 144–156
Clarkson, Thomas 17
class 138, 141–142. *See also* colour code
cohabitation 73, 94–98, 100–102, 139, 172
colonialism 2–3, 83–89, 99–105, 133, 133–134
colour code 15, 105–107, 113–118, 133–143, 144–156, 178
colour consciousness 18, 27, 90–98. *See also* Caribbean, and colour pyramid
  and 'passing' 119–126, 128
  historical roots 108–118
colour prejudice 75–76, 127–128. *See also* colour consciousness, injustice,
      and discrimination
colour pyramid 93, 99–107, 124–125, 142–143
Commonwealth 1–15, 27, 80
Coran, Giles 2
Critical Race Theory 156
Cugoano, Ottobah 11

D

Darwinism (cultural) 83
discrimination 35, 85–88, 113–114, 123–124, 127–132, 144–156. *See also* injustice, and racism

E

education 24, 33–34, 154
  in London 33–35, 36
employment. *See under* West Indians
Equiano, Olaudah 11–12, 17

F

family dynamics 54–63, 97, 99. *See also* Caribbean family life
Floyd, George viii, 16–17, 17, 139, 173

H

healing 150–151
history, attitudes to 12, 88–89, 110, 138
  and polarisation 147–148
human character 27–28, 144–146

I

immigration iv, 18–20, 19–20, 26–27, 40–46, 61
  and Africans 61–63
injustice 12–14, 35–36, 76, 90–98, 125–126, 150–151, 172–173. *See also* Caribbean, and under justice
  and compensation 17–18. *See also* justice and reparations
integration 40–52, 53–59

J

justice 131. *See also* injustice
  and compensation 12, 17–18, 109, 141
  and reparations 4, 82
  and the police x

K

King, Martin Luther 52, 121

**ADDRESSING THE LEGACY OF COLONIAL SLAVERY
AND INDUSTRIAL EXPLOITATION**

MJR is a UK Registered Charity no. 1161441

MJR's aim is to raise awareness of the legacies of colonial slavery
and industrial exploitation by gathering existing and commissioning
new research, making the findings known through educational
projects and seeking to resolve injustice, promote well-being and
encourage community reconciliation in new and innovative ways.

For more information see the MJR website: www.mjr-uk.com

Or contact MJR by email: info@mjr-uk.com
Join in on Twitter: @mjr_uk
Donate to MJR: tinyurl.com/donateMJR

BRINGING THE UNCHANGING WORD OF GOD TO A CHANGING WORLD

*The tribe of Issachar understood the times and knew
what Israel should do. (1 Chron 12:32)*

Issachar Ministries UK is a UK Registered Charity no. 1192583

Issachar Ministries UK / C and M Ministries helped launch MJR in
2015 and have been closely associated and supportive since then.

Issachar Ministries UK will be distributing both hard copies and
downloads from the Resources page on their website
https://www.issacharministries.co.uk/landingpage/

Or contact Issachar Ministries UK: Bedford Heights, Brickhill Drive,
Bedford, MK41 7PH
Email: info@issacharministries.co.uk
Telephone the office: 0333 090 2187 Tuesday to Friday 9am – 5pm